Cordon Bleu

Summer
Desserts

Cordon Bleu

Summer
Desserts

SPHERE BOOKS LIMITED
30/32 Grays Inn Road, London, WC1X 8JL

First published in Great Britain in 1972 by
B.P.C. Publishing Ltd.

© B.P.C. Publishing Ltd., 1972

First Sphere edition 1973

Designed by Melvyn Kyte
Printed by Proost, Turnhout, Belgium

ISBN 0 7221 2511 9

These recipes have been adapted from the Cordon Bleu Cookery Course
published by Purnell in association with the London Cordon Bleu Cookery
School
Principal Rosemary Hume ; Co-Principal Muriel Downes
Quantities given are enough for 4 servings.
Spoon measures are level unless otherwise stated.

Contents

Introduction

Light and fresh, that is the key-note for summer desserts. No more heavy puddings and rich sauces, those are for the colder months when we tend to be less active ; instead, guests and family like mousses, ices and, above all, fresh fruit. Cool, refreshing desserts are a must for meals at home, and can turn an ordinary picnic into a celebration occasion.

The fun of cooking at this time of the year will be all the greater if the family joins in, picking the fruit in the garden or lanes, and preparing it for the table. And you may find the children surprisingly willing, for who would not rather hull strawberries than peel potatoes ?

The secret of summer cooking, though, is in not sickening of a particular fruit because it happens to be in season. With this book we hope to help you ring the changes. One of the rules to remember is that if fruit is perfect it is best served whole — the visual pleasure of a dish of full firm fruit is at least equivalent enjoyment to an extra helping ! But if the fruit is less than perfect, that is the time to disguise its shape and use it for flavour alone.

Of course there are times even in summer when there is little good fruit around — especially if there has been a lot of rain. Then there is no reason why you should not still use chocolate, coffee, nuts, or any of the other year-round favourites. We have included a few of these recipes and you can always turn back to our **Winter Puddings** book for more ideas.

So enjoy your summer cooking. Don't give up entertaining because you feel it isn't the season — take your chance to give guests something they could not have at a winter dinner party.

Rosemary Hume
Muriel Downes

Fresh fruit sweets

English gardens and markets overflow with delicious fruits in the summer. Strawberries, gooseberries, raspberries, currants, cherries, plums — eat them raw or make them into delectable sweets. But remember some fruits, notably currants, are more palatable when cooked.

Cherries are the first to appear, imported from France and Italy in May and early June, then our own ripen and are followed by strawberries, then currants, raspberries and peaches. Towards the end of August and into September there are damsons, plums, new apples and the

hedgerow fruits — blackberries, bilberries and others. Imported melons and pineapples are plentiful right through from April to November.

One delicious sweet is sugared fruit — for this the fruit must be really ripe and can be a mixture of currants, raspberries, strawberries, stoned cherries, or whatever you wish. Pick the fruit over well and layer in a glass or china bowl, sprinkling each layer liberally with fine sugar. Cover with a plate and refrigerate for several hours before serving. By then the sugar will have melted to a rich syrup. Serve with cream and a crusty top sponge.

Just once a year, too, every family should have a summer pudding — see our recipes on pages 24 and 25.

Apples and pears were at one time a winter standby. But now, with better transport from overseas and better storage methods in the fruit and vegetable industry, lots of varieties are available right through the year. If you are cooking them, though, do remember that both turn brown if peeled and left exposed to the air; soaking in salt water does prevent this, but it spoils the flavour so it is better to prepare the fruit immediately before cooking — and do cook it thoroughly or it will still discolour.

Although we have called this section 'Fresh fruit sweets' don't forget that many of the creams, mousses and other sweets in this book will include fruit. The section on how to poach fruit is particularly useful for all types of recipe.

Strawberries Cordon Bleu 1

1 lb strawberries
6-8 sugar lumps
1 large orange
1 small glass brandy (2 fl oz)

Method
Hull the strawberries and place them in a bowl. Rub the lumps of sugar over the rind of the orange until they are soaked with oil, then squeeze the juice from the orange. Crush the sugar cubes and mix them with the orange juice and brandy. Pour this syrup over the strawberries, place a plate on top and chill thoroughly (2-3 hours) before serving.

Strawberries Cordon Bleu 2

1 lb strawberries
$\frac{1}{4}$ lb ratafias, or 2 macaroons
1 orange
1 tablespoon caster sugar
$\frac{1}{4}$ pint double cream

Method
Hull the strawberries and place them in a bowl with the ratafias (or macaroons broken in 3-4 pieces.) Grate the rind of the orange on the finest side of the grater, taking care not to remove any pith. Squeeze juice from the orange and pour half over the strawberries. Put the grated rind and remaining orange juice in a small basin, add the sugar and stir until dissolved. Whip the cream, sweeten with this orange syrup and pile on top of the strawberries. Chill for 1 hour before serving.

Strawberries Cordon Bleu 3

1 lb strawberries
1 orange
2 tablespoons caster sugar
$\frac{1}{4}$ pint double cream

Method
Hull the strawberries and place them in a bowl. Grate the rind of the orange on the finest side of the grater, taking particular care not to remove any pith. Squeeze the juice from half the orange and put it in a small basin with the sugar and rind; stir with a wooden spoon until the sugar melts.

Lightly whip the cream, fold into the orange syrup, then spoon this mixture over the strawberries. Cover and chill for 30 minutes before serving.

Strawberries maison

$1\frac{1}{2}$ lb strawberries
3-4 tablespoons muscat syrup
  (see page 117)
$\frac{1}{2}$ pint double cream (whipped)

Method
Hull the strawberries, then moisten them well with the muscat syrup. Chill and serve with whipped cream.

Strawberry tabatières

½ lb strawberries
6 tablespoons redcurrant glaze
¼ pint double cream

For choux pastry
3 oz butter
7½ fl oz water
3¾ oz plain flour (sifted)
3 eggs

For pastry cream
1 egg (separated)
1 egg yolk
2 oz caster sugar
2-3 drops of vanilla essence
¾ oz plain flour
½ oz cornflour
½ pint milk

For praline
2 oz almonds (unblanched)
2 oz caster sugar

Method

Set oven at 400°F or Mark 6.

First make choux pastry: boil butter and water together, draw pan aside, allow bubbles to subside, then shoot in all the flour at once. Stir the mixture vigorously until it is smooth. Cool it slightly, then beat in the eggs thoroughly, one at a time. The dough should then be smooth and glossy. Pipe out the choux on to a dampened baking sheet in the shape of small turnovers and bake in pre-set oven for about 20 minutes, until crisp to the touch.

To prepare pastry cream: cream the egg yolks, sugar and vanilla essence together until the mixture looks white; add the flours and a little cold milk and make into a smooth paste. Heat the remaining milk and pour it on to the egg mixture, blend together and return to pan. Stir cream over the heat until boiling, then draw pan aside. Stiffly whip the egg white.

Turn one-third of the pastry cream into a bowl, fold in the egg white gradually, then return mixture to the pan containing the remaining cream and stir gently over heat for 2-3 minutes to set the egg white. Turn cream into a bowl, cover and leave to cool.

To make praline: put almonds and sugar into a small, heavy pan; cook over a low heat and stir with a metal spoon when the sugar begins to colour. Continue stirring while the sugar dissolves and turns a good deep brown. The praline is ready when the nuts are well toasted (beginning to crackle). Turn praline on to an oiled baking sheet and leave to cool; then crush with a rolling pin, or use a nut mill or cheese grater.

Lightly whip cream and fold it into the pastry cream, adding enough praline to flavour it well. Split the cold choux pastry and fill with the praline cream. Arrange the strawberries, dipped in or brushed with warm red-currant glaze, round the edge of each 'tabatière'. Then arrange on serving dish.

> **Tabatière** is the French word for a snuff-box, snuff being 'tabac (tobacco) à prise'. This recipe is so called because the choux pastry is folded into a turn-over shape, similar to that of a tobacco pouch.

Strawberries in raspberry cream

1 lb strawberries
caster sugar (for dusting)
juice of $\frac{1}{2}$ orange
1-2 tablespoons kirsch
$\frac{1}{2}$ lb raspberries
4 tablespoons icing sugar
$\frac{1}{2}$ pint double cream

Method

Hull the strawberries, place them in a bowl, dust with the caster sugar and sprinkle with the orange juice and kirsch; cover bowl and leave in a cool place while preparing cream.

To prepare raspberry cream: rub raspberries through a nylon sieve and work the icing sugar into this purée, a little at a time. Lightly whip the cream, carefully fold in the sweetened raspberry cream and spoon this over the strawberries.

Strawberry Condé

1 lb strawberries
3 tablespoons Carolina rice
1 pint milk
1 vanilla pod
$1\frac{1}{2}$ oz caster sugar
scant $\frac{1}{2}$ oz gelatine
2 tablespoons cold water
juice of 1 orange
$2\frac{1}{2}$ fl oz double cream (lightly whipped)
1 egg white
extra cream for decoration (optional)

6-inch diameter tin, or charlotte mould ($1\frac{1}{2}$ pints capacity)

Method

Lightly oil the mould. Wash the rice and cook slowly in the milk, with vanilla pod to flavour, until it is tender (about 45 minutes). Remove vanilla pod, add the sugar and allow the rice to cool.

Soften the gelatine in 2 tablespoons cold water, add to the orange juice in a pan and dissolve over gentle heat, then add liquid to the rice. Fold in the cream and lastly the stiffly-whisked egg white. Pour the mixture into the mould and chill in refrigerator for 2-3 hours. When set turn out the strawberry Condé into a serving dish. Mask the top with cream and surround with strawberries, or serve them separately as a compote sprinkled with orange juice and sugar.

> **Condé** is the name given to a set rice cream, but is frequently used to decribe a sweet dish featuring rice.

Brazilian bananas

8 bananas
2 tablespoons rum
2 dessertspoons instant coffee
2 dessertspoons caster sugar
8 fl oz double cream
few almonds (browned, flaked)

Method
Peel the bananas, slice thickly into a serving dish or coupe glasses and sprinkle over the rum. Dissolve the coffee in 3-4 tablespoons boiling water, add caster sugar, leave until cold.

Whip the cream and add the cold coffee mixture. Cover the bananas with the coffee-flavoured cream, scatter a few browned flaked almonds on top and serve chilled.

Brazilian bananas, topped with coffee cream and flaked almonds

Banana coupe

8 bananas
½ pint double cream
4 dessertspoons strawberry jam

Method
Turn the cream into a cold basin and whip it with a fork or a small whisk until it is thick enough just to hold its shape when a little is left on the fork or whisk.

Put the strawberry jam in the bottom of coupe or sundae glasses. Peel the bananas and cut them in thick, slanting slices, dropping these straight into the glasses as you cut them.

Spoon over the cream to cover all the slices of banana.

How to poach fruit

A compote is the term for fresh or dried fruit which is cooked, whole or cut into quarters, in a thick or thin syrup ; various flavourings may be added to this syrup. So often fruit is just put in a pan with water to cover, an unknown or variable amount of sugar is thrown in and the whole is cooked rather haphazardly. The resulting dish is usually dismissed as 'only stewed fruit', a justified criticism if it is over-cooked and mushy, with a watery syrup. Fruits best suited for making compotes are apricots, plums and forced rhubarb.

Preparation of fruit

Pick over fruit to remove any damaged or mouldy flesh, then wash it in a colander under a running tap.

Apricots and large plums. Split by running a stainless steel knife round the fruit from the stalk end, following the slight indentation and cutting through to the stone. By giving the fruit a slight twist the halves should separate easily and the stone can be removed. A few stones can be cracked and the kernels added to the compote.

If the stone will not come away, cook fruit whole and detach stone after cooking.

Place the fruit, rounded side down, in a pan with syrup and bring very slowly to boil. Allow syrup to boil up and over fruit and then reduce heat, cover pan and leave to simmer very gently until tender.

Even fully ripe fruit must be thoroughly cooked to allow the syrup to penetrate, sweeten and prevent discolouration.

Rhubarb. Wash and dry 1-1$\frac{1}{2}$ lb rhubarb and cut into even lengths. Spread 2 tablespoons of redcurrant jelly or strained raspberry jam over the bottom and sides of a casserole. Put the rhubarb on this and put 1 more tablespoon of jelly or jam on top. Cover and cook in a moderate oven at 350°F or Mark 4 for about 45 minutes, or until tender.

Rhubarb can also be cut in even lengths and cooked as for apricots and plums.

Syrup. The most important point to remember when cooking fruit is that the water and sugar should first be made into a syrup. An average proportion for this syrup is 3 rounded tablespoons of granulated sugar to $\frac{1}{2}$ pint water per lb of fruit. Heat gently in a pan to dissolve sugar, boil rapidly for 2 minutes before the fruit is added. The syrup may be flavoured with pared lemon rind or a vanilla pod.

Watchpoint Do not add any extra sugar with the fruit even if it is very sour, because too thick a syrup tends to toughen the skins of some fruit while cooking. If the fruit is excessively sour, it is better to add a little extra sugar when the fruit is tender and still hot.

Pears pralinées

4-5 ripe even-size dessert pears
light sugar syrup (made with 1 cup
   granulated sugar, 2 cups water
   and ½ split vanilla pod or few drops
   vanilla essence)
stale sponge cake (preferably
   Victoria sponge, or Madeira cake)
Grand Marnier, or kirsch
   (optional)

For praline
2 oz unblanched almonds
good 2 oz caster sugar

For cream
½ pint double cream
1 egg white (whipped)
caster sugar (to sweeten)

Peeling pears, leaving stalks on,
and placing them in the pan of syrup

Method

First prepare the syrup by mixing the ingredients together in a pan, simmer for 5 minutes then remove vanilla pod. Peel and core the pears, leaving on the stalks, and place them in the syrup. Cover the pan and poach for 10-15 minutes with the lid on. When pears are tender, leave them in the syrup until quite cold.

Meanwhile prepare the praline. Put the almonds and sugar together in a small heavy saucepan; cook over gentle heat, allowing the sugar to melt and begin to brown before stirring with a metal spoon. When the almonds are caramelised, continue to cook for 1-2 minutes to ensure that they are thoroughly toasted through. Turn caramel out on to an oiled tin and leave to set, then grind through a cheese grater or nutmill and keep in a screw-top jar until needed.

Stamp out a round of sponge cake to fit each pear; set these on a dish and moisten with a little of the syrup and sprinkle, if wished, with a little Grand Marnier (or kirsch). Drain the pears, set each on a round of cake and dish up. Whip the cream lightly, add it to the egg white, sweeten slightly and stir in 2-3 tablespoons of the praline. Pile this on top of the pears, sprinkle over a little extra praline and chill before serving.

Pears Charcot

4 ripe dessert pears
$\frac{1}{2}$ pint water
3 tablespoons granulated sugar
juice of $\frac{1}{2}$ lemon
2 tablespoons smooth apricot jam
$\frac{1}{2}$ lb quince jam

For vanilla cream
$\frac{3}{4}$ pint milk
1 vanilla pod, or 2-3 drops of
  vanilla essence
3 egg yolks
2 tablespoons caster sugar
$\frac{1}{2}$ oz gelatine (softened in 5
  tablespoons water)
$\frac{1}{4}$ pint double cream (lightly
  whipped)

*Deep 5-6 inch diameter cake tin,
or soufflé dish (No 2 size), or
8-inch diameter sandwich tin*

*After scooping out centre of pears,
place them immediately, rounded
side down, in the pan of hot syrup*

Method

Lightly oil the tin or soufflé dish. Put the water, sugar and lemon juice in a pan over gentle heat. When the sugar has dissolved, boil for 3 minutes. Meanwhile peel the pears, cut in half, scoop out the core with a teaspoon and immediately place pear halves, rounded side down, in the hot syrup. Cover the pan and poach pears carefully for 15-20 minutes; leave them to cool in the pan.

To make vanilla cream: heat the milk to scalding point with the vanilla pod (or vanilla essence), cover pan and leave milk to infuse until it is well flavoured. Cream egg yolks thoroughly with the sugar, and add the milk (first taking out the vanilla pod); blend liquid well, return it to the pan and stir over gentle heat until the custard coats the back of the wooden spoon, then strain and leave it to cool.

Melt the gelatine mixture over gentle heat, and add it to the custard. Tip the custard into a thin saucepan and stand this in a bowl of cold water (for quickness, add a little ice to water). Stir until custard begins to thicken creamily, then fold in half the whipped cream.

Turn the mixture into prepared tin or soufflé dish and leave to set (about 2 hours). Lift the pears out of the syrup and keep on one side; add the jams to the syrup in the pan, melt slowly and then boil for 2-3 minutes. Allow syrup sauce to cool.

Turn the vanilla cream on to a serving dish and decorate with the remaining cream. Arrange the pears round the cream and coat them with the sauce.

Pears in red wine

5-6 ripe dessert pears
5 oz lump sugar
$\frac{1}{4}$ pint water
$\frac{1}{4}$ pint red wine (claret or
   burgundy)
strip of lemon rind
small piece of stick cinnamon
1 teaspoon arrowroot
1 oz almonds
whipped cream (optional)

Method

To make syrup: dissolve sugar, water, wine, lemon rind and cinnamon slowly in a pan. Bring to boil and boil for 1 minute.

Keeping stalks on pears, remove peel and the 'eye' from each base and place in the prepared syrup. Poach pears in the pan, covered, until tender. Even if pears are ripe, you must allow at least 20-30 minutes to prevent them discolouring around cores. Remove pears and strain syrup, which should be reduced to $\frac{1}{2}$ pint in the cooking.

Mix the arrowroot with a little water before adding to syrup and stir until boiling; then cook until liquid is clear.

Meanwhile shred and brown almonds: blanch, skin and split; cut each half lengthways in fine pieces and brown quickly in the oven at 350°F or Mark 4.

Arrange pears in a serving dish. Spoon over the wine sauce and finish by scattering the browned and shredded almonds on top.

Serve cold, handing a bowl of whipped cream separately.

The cooked pears take on a rich red colour from the wine

Pears in orange cream

4-6 ripe pears
$\frac{1}{2}$ pint water
3 tablespoons granulated sugar

For custard
$\frac{1}{2}$ pint milk
2 egg yolks
1 teaspoon arrowroot
1 teaspoon caster sugar

For orange cream
1 large orange
5 sugar lumps
$\frac{1}{4}$ pint double cream

Method

Peel and halve the pears and scoop out cores with a teaspoon. Place pears at once in the water, with the sugar, rounded side down. Cook gently until pears are tender and leave to cool in syrup.

Remove outer rind from half the orange, shred, and cook in boiling water until tender. Drain and rinse well with cold water.

To prepare custard: scald milk in a pan; cream egg yolks, arrowroot and sugar in a bowl until light. Tip on milk and return to the pan. Stir over a gentle heat until custard coats the back of a spoon, but do not boil. Strain and allow to cool.

Rub the lump sugar over the other half of orange to remove all the zest (each lump should be saturated with the oil from the skin). Place these lumps in a small basin and pour over 5 tablespoons of strained orange juice; stir until sugar is dissolved. Lightly whip the cream, stir in the orange syrup and the cold custard.

Drain pears, dish up and coat with the orange cream. Sprinkle over the prepared orange rind.

Macaroons à l'orange

1 packet of macaroons (allow 1 per person)
curaçao, or Grand Marnier
$\frac{1}{2}$ ripe pear (Doyenne de Comice), or $\frac{1}{2}$-1 ripe peach

For orange cream
1 orange
6-8 sugar lumps
$\frac{1}{2}$ pint double cream
little caster sugar (optional)

The dry, Continental type macaroons are best for this dish.

Method

Spread the macaroons out on a dish and sprinkle well with the liqueur; leave for 5-10 minutes.

Meanwhile rub the sugar lumps over the orange until they are well soaked with oil. Crush them and stir in 1-2 tablespoons of juice from the orange. Then whip the cream lightly, adding the orange syrup gradually, and adding extra sugar to taste, if wished. The cream should be thick enough to coat easily, but be careful not to overwhip it.

Dish up the macaroons on individual plates, top each with a section of pear (or peach), then coat with the orange cream.

Pears with damsons

8 ripe dessert pears
½ lb damsons, or 1 lb damson
  cheese (see right)
8 oz granulated sugar
¾ pint water
1 vanilla pod
¼ pint double cream (to decorate)

Method

Put the sugar in a pan with the water and vanilla pod and dissolve over gentle heat, then boil steadily for 5 minutes to make 1 pint sugar syrup. Remove vanilla pod.

Peel the pears and remove the core from the flower end with the point of a potato peeler but keep on stalks. Poach pears in the syrup for 15 minutes.

Watchpoint Do not decrease this time even if the pears are ripe as they must be soaked with syrup to prevent them discolouring when cool. Drain the pears from the syrup, put them in a dish and leave to cool.

Wash and stone the damsons, put them in the pan of syrup and simmer gently until they are tender. Turn into a strainer and allow to drain, then rub the damsons (now pulpy) through strainer. Dilute with a little of the syrup to give a good coating consistency. Chill well. Strain this purée over the pears. Whip the cream stiffly and pipe a thick ruff around edge of the dish.

Damson cheese

4 lb damsons
about 2 pints water
1 lb granulated sugar to every
  pound of purée

Method

Wash the fruit, put into a small preserving pan or a thick stewpan and pour in just enough water to come level with the fruit. Bring slowly to the boil and simmer gently until the fruit is thoroughly soft and pulpy. Stir occasionally. While it is cooking, remove any stones that come to the surface. Push the pulp through a sieve or put into a blender, then weigh it and weigh out an equal amount of sugar. Clean out the pan, return both pulp and sugar to the pan, dissolve over low heat, then boil gently until very thick (35-40 minutes), stirring constantly. Towards the end of the cooking, stir more frequently to avoid any possibility of sticking. The cheese is done when a wooden spoon drawn through the centre leaves the mixture separated so as to show the bottom of the pan. Have ready small, warmed jars or pots. Fill them with the purée, leave until cold, then tie down.

Other fruit cheeses are made in the same way. Remember to add just sufficient water to enable the fruit to be cooked to a pulp. The reason for choosing a preserving or shallow pan is that a certain amount of evaporation must take place, especially when the fruit has been pulped and the sugar added.

Raspberries in Melba sauce

1 lb raspberries
4 tablespoons icing sugar

Method
Make a raspberry purée by rubbing one-third of the raspberries through a nylon sieve. Sift the icing sugar and beat it into the raspberry purée a little at a time. Pour this sauce over the whole raspberries and leave them for at least one hour before serving.

Raspberries in strawberry cream

8-12 oz raspberries
$\frac{1}{4}$ pint double cream
$\frac{1}{4}$ pint sweetened strawberry purée
crystallised violets (for decoration)

Method
Arrange the raspberries in coupe glasses. Whip the cream lightly until it just begins to thicken, then add the strawberry purée, a little at a time, and continue whipping until the cream holds its shape. Spoon this over the raspberries and decorate with crystallised violets.

To make a strawberry purée rub the hulled strawberries through a nylon sieve, or blend them in a liquidiser. Add icing, or caster, sugar to taste.

Raspberry suédoise

1 lb raspberries (fresh, or frozen without sugar)
sugar syrup (made with 4 oz granulated sugar and $\frac{1}{4}$ pint water)
1 oz gelatine (softened in $\frac{1}{4}$ pint water)
tiny meringues (made with 1 egg white and 2 oz caster sugar — see method page 144)
$\frac{1}{2}$ pint double cream (flavoured with vanilla essence)

6-inch diameter top (No. 2 size) soufflé dish

Method
To make the sugar syrup, heat sugar and water gently in a pan to dissolve sugar, then boil rapidly for 2 minutes. Leave to cool.

Make a purée of the raspberries in a blender, then rub them through a nylon sieve to remove the seeds. Sweeten purée with the sugar syrup, measure out $1\frac{1}{2}$ pints, making up quantity with water. Dissolve the softened gelatine over heat and add this liquid to the fruit mixture. When quite cold, pour liquid into the wet soufflé dish and leave it to set. Then turn suédoise on to a serving dish, cover it with the whipped cream and meringues.

Raspberry and redcurrant cheese

1 lb raspberries
$\frac{1}{2}$ lb redcurrants
$\frac{3}{4}$ lb granulated sugar
$\frac{1}{2}$ pint water
gelatine (see method)
$\frac{1}{4}$ pint double cream (whipped)

Ring mould (1½-2 pints capacity)

Method
Put the raspberries and red-currants into a saucepan with the sugar and $\frac{1}{2}$ pint of water. Stir over gentle heat until sugar is dissolved, then rub through a nylon strainer. Measure fruit purée and allow $\frac{3}{4}$ oz of gelatine to each pint of purée.

Soak gelatine in a little water (use 3 tablespoons water for every $\frac{3}{4}$ oz). Add the soaked gelatine to the hot fruit purée and stir until gelatine is dissolved. Pour into a wet ring mould and leave to set. Turn out and serve with whipped cream piled in the centre.

Summer pudding 1

$1\frac{1}{2}$ lb mixed fruit — currants, raspberries, stoned red cherries, etc. (picked over)
5-6 rounds of stale white sandwich loaf
4-6 oz granulated sugar

Pudding basin (1½ pints capacity)

Use an uncut sandwich loaf, if possible, rather than sliced bread which is too doughy and makes for a sodden pudding.

The fruit should weigh $1\frac{1}{2}$ lb when picked over. To allow for the stalks etc. begin with 2 lb mixed fruit.

Method
Remove crusts from bread and cut 1-2 slices to fit the bottom of the basin. Arrange slices to line the sides, cutting them if necessary and reserving two slices. Put the fruit and sugar into a shallow pan, cover and set on a low heat for 10-15 minutes, shaking pan occasionally. By this time the juice will have run and the fruit will be tender. Cool a little and adjust sweetening, if necessary.

Half fill the bread-lined basin with fruit, then put in one layer of bread and fill up with the fruit. Cover the fruit with bread and then spoon in just enough juice to fill the basin. Put a small plate on top, pressing it down on the bread and place a 2 lb weight on top. Stand basin on a plate to catch any juice that spills over. Refrigerate overnight, then turn out and serve with cream.

Summer pudding 2

1½-2 lb blackcurrants, or raspberries, or loganberries, or blackberries (picked over)
¼ pint water
approximately ½ sandwich loaf (thinly sliced)
granulated sugar (to taste)
arrowroot (slaked with fruit juice, or water)

6-inch diameter top (No. 2 size) soufflé dish, or pudding basin (1½ pints capacity)

Method

Put the fruit and water into a pan, cover and simmer for 4-5 minutes (1-2 minutes longer for currants); strain. Work the fruit in an electric blender with a little of the juice, or rub through a Mouli sieve. If blended, strain the pulp through a strainer to get rid of any tiny pips. Add the rest of the juice to the purée, sweeten well. Remove the crusts from the bread. Pour a little fruit purée into bottom of dish or bowl, put 1-2 slices of bread on top and add more of the purée. Continue like this until the dish is very full, making sure that each layer is well soaked with the purée. Reserve a good ¼ pint of purée for the sauce. Put a plate and a 2 lb weight on top of the pudding and leave overnight.

Add a little water to the reserved purée, add arrowroot, bring to the boil, stirring continuously, pour off and cool. Turn out pudding, spoon this sauce over it and serve with cream.

Boîte au chocolat aux fruits

3 eggs
4½ oz caster sugar
1 tablespoon boiling water
3 oz plain flour (sifted with
pinch of salt)

To finish
3 oz plain block chocolate
2-3 tablespoons rum, or kirsch,
or Grand Marnier
½ lb raspberries, or strawberries,
or 2-3 fresh peaches (sliced)
caster sugar (to sweeten fruit)
¼-½ pint double cream (whipped)

8-inch square cake tin

*Left : when chocolate is hard the
squares are removed from the
paper with a palette knife*
*Right : the sugared raspberries
are placed on top of the cake before
being covered with whipped cream*

Method
Set the oven at 350°F or Mark 4.
Grease and flour the cake tin.

Separate the eggs. Beat the
yolks thoroughly with half the
sugar and the boiling water in a
bowl over hot water. When
mixture is thick and mousse-like,
remove bowl from the heat.

Whisk the whites stiffly, then
whisk in the rest of the sugar ;
cut and fold this into the yolk
mixture with the sifted flour and
salt. Turn mixture at once into
prepared tin ; bake for about 25
minutes in pre-set moderate
oven. Turn cake out and cool.

Meanwhile break up the
chocolate and melt it over very
gentle heat, but do not allow the
chocolate itself to reach more
than blood heat (98°F). Spread
this evenly and moderately
thickly over a large square of
greaseproof paper and, when
just set, mark into small squares
(1¾ inches) with a sharp knife.
Leave in a cool airy room to
harden completely.

Sprinkle the cake well with the rum (or liqueur) and prepare the fruit. Then sugar the fruit and leave to stand for a short time. Spread the sides of the cake with cream. Peel the chocolate squares off the paper and press them round sides of cake, slightly overlapping. Top edge of squares should come above top of cake. Fill cake with fruit and pile more cream on top.

Pêches farcies

4 ripe cling peaches
12 ratafias
1 tablespoon Grand Marnier, or curaçao
grated rind and juice of $\frac{1}{2}$ orange
1 tablespoon caster sugar
$\frac{1}{4}$ pint double cream

This can also be presented in a slightly different way by using kirsch to soak the ratafias and Melba sauce (see right) instead of cream to coat the peaches.

Method
Halve and peel the peaches. Crumble ratafias and soak them in the liqueur. Fill into each peach and reshape by putting the two halves together. Mix the grated orange rind and juice with sugar and stir until the sugar dissolves. Whip the cream and, as it begins to thicken, carefully add the orange syrup. Spoon this over the peaches and serve.

Pêches Melba

4 ripe cling peaches
4 tablespoons granulated sugar
$\frac{1}{2}$ pint water
$\frac{1}{2}$ vanilla pod
1 pint vanilla cream ice (see page 58)
3-4 fl oz Chantilly cream (see page 153)

For Melba sauce
8 oz fresh, or frozen, raspberries
4-5 tablespoons sifted icing sugar

4 coupe glasses

Method
Prepare a syrup with the sugar, water and vanilla pod (see page 15). Peel and halve the peaches, remove stones and put the peaches, rounded side down, in the syrup to poach. (This will take at least 10 minutes.)
Watchpoint The peaches must be ripe. To test if a yellow clingstone peach is ripe, rub the skin gently with the blade of a table knife; if the fruit is ripe, the skin will peel off very easily. If it doesn't, do not scald the peaches, but simply cut them in half and poach with the skin on. When the fruit is cooked the skin will be easy to peel off.

Allow the peaches to cool in the syrup, then drain. Prepare the Melba sauce by rubbing the raspberries through a nylon strainer and beating the icing sugar into this purée a little at a time until the mixture thickens. Chill.

Just before serving, place a scoop of vanilla cream ice in each coupe glass, arrange two peach halves over it, coat with a tablespoon of Melba sauce and decorate with a rosette of Chantilly cream.

Sweet raspberry purée, vanilla cream ice and Chantilly cream are added to peaches poached in syrup for Pêches Melba, served in coupe glasses

Melon and pawpaw cocktail

2 small melons
1 pawpaw
juice of ½ lemon

Choose green-fleshed melon such as Ogen or Honeydew to give a better contrast with the pawpaw.

Method
Cut the pawpaw in ½-inch cubes and squeeze over the lemon juice. Halve the melons, scoop out the seeds and fill the centre with the prepared pawpaw.

Melon en surprise

1 Cantaloupe, or Honeydew, melon
4-6 oz redcurrants
½ lb raspberries
3-4 tablespoons caster sugar
1 glass sherry
½ egg white (lightly beaten)

Method
Select about 6 of the best sprays of redcurrants and keep them on one side for frosting if you wish to use them for decoration (see opposite page).

Cut the top off the melon, carefully scoop out the seeds and discard them. Remove the flesh in balls with a vegetable scoop (much the same effect can be obtained with the bowl of a teaspoon; however, the pieces of melon will then be more egg-shaped than like marbles).

String the redcurrants and pick over the raspberries. Macer-

Scooping out balls of melon flesh with a vegetable scoop ; a teaspoon can also be used to give much the same effect

ate the fruit by placing it in a bowl or plastic container and sprinkling over the sugar and sherry. Cover it tighly and place it in the refrigerator to chill for 1-2 hours. Tie the melon shell in a polythene bag and chill.

Watchpoint It is most important to cover the melon very carefully when chilling in a refrigerator, or you will soon find that its penetrating smell and flavour is absorbed by any other uncovered food, particularly dairy produce and bacon.

Meanwhile frost the reserved redcurrants by brushing the strings of currants very sparingly with egg white, rolling them in caster sugar and leaving to dry on a wire cake rack.

Take chilled fruit from refrigerator and pile it back into the melon skin and top with a little crown or wreath of frosted currants or a few reserved raspberries (as in photograph). Set the melon on a dessert plate, lined with vine leaves, or any decorative leaves.

Serve with a selection of friandises (or petits fours).

Melon en surprise : in goblet are macaroons à l'orange and muscadins

Compote of cherries

1½-2 lb red cherries
3 rounded tablespoons granulated
  sugar
good pinch of cinnamon
1 tablespoon arrowroot
approximately ¼ pint water

Method

Stone the cherries and put into a large pan with sugar and cinnamon. Cover pan and set on a low heat until the juice runs freely (about 7-10 minutes); by this time cherries will be at boiling point. Draw pan aside.

Slake the arrowroot with a little of the cold water, add to the pan and shake. Add remaining water (see note below). Bring cherries to the boil again and turn into a serving dish.

Note : cherries are best stewed quickly this way because in prolonged cooking their skins become toughened. The addition of arrowroot here does make for a smoother and richer-looking compote, but the result should not be gluey. The amount of water which should be added varies according to juiciness of cherries. Use your discretion, remembering that a compote should be rich-looking and -tasting and full of fruit.

Stoning cherries. This should be done before cooking. The best and simplest implement to use is a small, pea-sized vegetable scoop. Alternatively, try the point of a potato peeler, or the bent end of a hairpin. Insert your implement at the stalk hole, give a twist and draw out the stone.

Cherry strudel

For strudel dough
10 oz plain flour
pinch of salt
1 egg (beaten)
¼ pint luke-warm water
little butter (melted)
icing sugar (for dusting)

For filling
2 lb Morello cherries
4 oz cake, or bread, crumbs
1 teaspoon cinnamon
8 oz caster sugar
4 oz ground almonds

Method

Sift the flour and salt into a mixing bowl. Add the egg to the flour with the warm water. Mix until smooth, turn on to a pastry board and knead and beat until elastic. This is done by repeatedly picking up the dough and throwing it down on to the board until it is smooth and shiny and leaves the hand cleanly. Put in a floured basin, cover and leave in a warm place for 15 minutes.

Meanwhile, prepare the filling. Stone the cherries and mix together with other ingredients. Set aside.

Set the oven at 400°F or Mark 6. Roll the pastry on a floured cloth and then pull gently from all sides until paper-thin. Brush well with melted butter and, using scissors, trim ½ inch from all round the edge.

Fill with cherry mixture, roll up and bake in pre-set oven for 30 minutes until crisp and golden. Dust with icing sugar when slightly cooled.

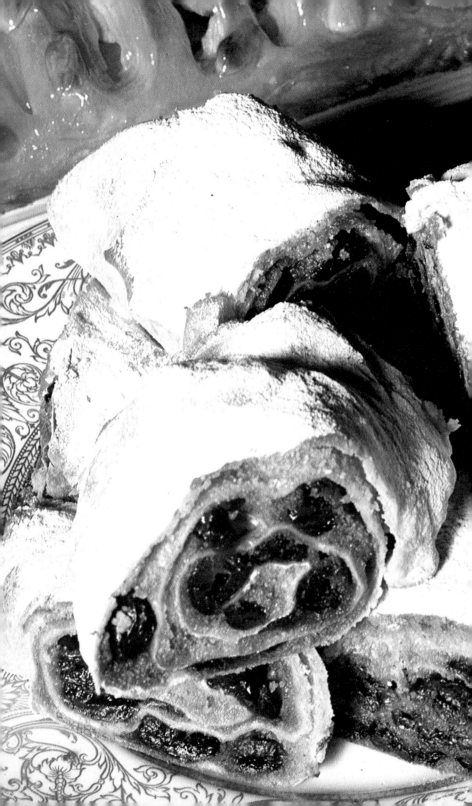

Cherries Montmorency

(Compote with orange cream and macaroons)

compote of 1½-2 lb fine, large, red
cherries (chilled) — see page 32

For macaroons
4 oz ground almonds
8 oz caster sugar
2 egg whites
2-3 drops of vanilla, or almond,
essence
½ oz rice flour, or plain flour

For orange cream
3-4 sugar lumps
1 orange
approximately ½ pint double
cream
2 tablespoons kirsch (optional)

*Forcing bag and plain pipe; rice
paper (optional)*

Method

Set the oven at 325-350°F
or Mark 3-4. First prepare the
macaroons. Work the almonds
and sugar well together, or
pound them, if preferred, to
extract as much oil as possible.
Break the egg whites slightly
with a fork and add them by
degrees to the almond mixture,
creaming them well together.
(This may be done using the
paddle of an electric mixer.)
Then add the essence and
allow mixture to stand for 5-10
minutes. Fill macaroon mixture
into a forcing bag fitted with a
plain pipe, and pipe it out on to
rice paper or baking sheets
(lightly greased and floured).
Be careful to pipe so as to make
fairly flat rounds; this is helped
by banging the sheet lightly on
the table. Bake macaroons in the
pre-set oven for 12-15 minutes
or until well cracked and a light
colour. A good macaroon
must not be browned or over-
baked. Take them from the oven
and leave to cool.

Rub the lumps of sugar on the
rind of the orange until they are
well impregnated with oil.
Crush them in a bowl and add
the strained juice of the orange.
Whip the cream lightly until it
will barely hold its shape, then
fold in the orange syrup.

Arrange the macaroons and
the cherry compote, free of
juice, in layers in a serving
dish. Large macaroons may
be broken into 2-3 pieces;
sprinkle macaroons with kirsch
if wished. Spoon orange cream
over top, make sure that it is
not too solid but will run over
and into the pudding nicely.
This sweet resembles a trifle.

Rich cherry compote

1½ lb fresh (or canned) Morello, or
  dark red, cherries
1 tablespoon granulated sugar
pinch of ground cinnamon
1 wineglass red wine
2-3 tablespoons redcurrant jelly
  (preferably home-made — see
  page 155)
grated rind and juice of 1 orange
1 dessertspoon-1 tablespoon
  arrowroot (slaked with 1-2
  tablespoons water)

This may be served hot or cold
with either cream sweets, rich
game or poultry.

Method
Stone the cherries and put into
a pan with the granulated sugar
and the cinnamon. Cover pan
and heat until the juice runs
from the cherries; this will be
practically at boiling point. Turn
fruit into a bowl. Put the wine in
the pan and reduce it to half
quantity, then add the redcurrant jelly, grated orange rind
and juice; heat gently until jelly
is melted. Add the juice from
cherries and slaked arrowroot.
Only add about 1 dessertspoon
of arrowroot to begin with.

Watchpoint If preferred, arrowroot may be omitted but
it does help to bind the liquid
slightly together. If using home-
made jelly, it may not dissolve
very readily, in which case run
the sauce through a strainer
before putting in the cherries.

Bring this to boiling point,
then draw pan aside and add
the cherries.

Plain cherry sauce

1 lb red cherries
2-3 tablespoons granulated
  sugar
pinch of ground cinnamon
approximately $\frac{1}{4}$ pint water
squeeze of lemon juice
  (optional)
1 dessertspoon arrowroot
1 tablespoon water

This cherry sauce is good with
any type of sponge pudding.

Method
Stone the cherries and put into
a pan with the sugar and cinnamon, cover and set on a low
heat until the juice runs freely,
then take cherries out with a
draining spoon. Add the water
to the juice, boil gently for 4-5
minutes and draw pan aside.
Taste for sweetness and adjust
accordingly; if too sweet, add a
squeeze of lemon juice.

Slake the arrowroot with 1
tablespoon water and add to
liquid. Bring back to the boil;
the liquid should be the consistency of cream. Replace the
cherries in pan, reheat them for
hot sauce.

Cherry pudding

1 lb red cherries (stoned)
2$\frac{1}{2}$ tablespoons caster sugår
$\frac{1}{2}$ pint milk
3 oz fresh white breadcrumbs
2 egg yolks
grated rind of $\frac{1}{2}$ lemon

For meringue topping
2 egg whites
4 oz caster sugar

*6-inch diameter (No. 2 size) soufflé
dish*

Fresh cherries should be used
for this pudding as canned ones
would be too sweet.

Method
Set oven at 350°F or Mark 4.

Place cherries in a pan, add
a light sprinkling of sugar, cover
and set on low heat for 2-3
minutes.

Meantime scald milk, pour
on to the breadcrumbs and after
5 minutes stir in the egg yolks,
remainder of sugar and grated
lemon rind. Add the cherries,
draining away any juice, and
turn mixture into dish; stand it
in a bain-marie and cook in the
pre-set oven until just set (approximately 30-40 minutes).
Remove the pudding from the
oven and turn heat down to
300°F or Mark 2.

To prepare meringue topping;
whip egg whites to a firm snow,
then beat in 1 teaspoon of the
weighed sugar. When the whites
are quite firm, quickly fold in the
remaining sugar. Pile meringue
mixture on top of the pudding,
dust with a little extra caster
sugar, leave for 4-5 minutes,
then put pudding into the oven
for 30 minutes. Serve hot or
cold with fresh cream.

Adding the drained cherries to the milk, egg and breadcrumb mixture before the preliminary cooking

Piling meringue on to the pudding, which then continues cooking until meringue is crisp (see below)

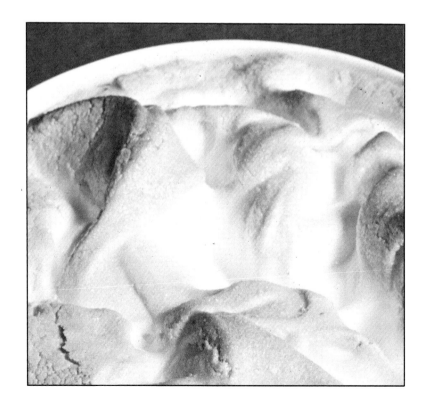

Pineapple en surprise

For pineapple
2 large pineapples
caster sugar
3-4 tablespoons kirsch
2 quarts orange water ice
  (see page 55)

For spun sugar
3 oz lump, or granulated, sugar
5 tablespoons water
pinch of cream of tartar

Sugar thermometer ; an oiled rolling pin, or oiled handle of a large wooden spoon ; 2 forks

This sweet is really for a special occasion and the quantities given are for 12 people.

Method

Cut the top off each pineapple and a small slice from the bottoms to make them stand firm. With a serrated-edged knife, carefully cut flesh out of pineapples in one piece ; cut it into slices and stamp out the hard core in the centre. Dust pineapple slices with sugar and moisten with the kirsch ; cover and leave in refrigerator until ready to serve. Wrap pineapple shells in foil or polythene bags and chill also.

To serve : set pineapple shells on a chilled dish, fill them with scoops of orange water ice and replace the tops. Surround shells with pineapple slices, decorate these with spun sugar, and serve with a selection of petits fours.

Spun sugar

This really belongs to the art of the confiseur. However, you can make a good imitation, providing you have 10 minutes to spare within 1 hour of serving dinner.

Put sugar and water into a small pan, dissolve it over gentle heat, then add cream of tartar. Boil mixture rapidly, occasionally brushing inside of pan with cold water to absorb any sugar crystals. Boil to 280°F, when the sugar will be a pale gold colour. Dip bottom of pan at once in cold water to stop the boiling ; set aside.

Cover floor nearby with 2-3 sheets of newspaper ; have ready the rolling pin, or if the wooden spoon is being used, stick the bowl end under a board or weight on table so that the handle projects over the floor.

Prop pan of syrup on a cloth to keep it steady, hold the two forks facing together and dip (don't stir) the prongs into syrup. Then, with a loose wrist movement, pass forks rapidly to and fro over the rolling pin (held in one hand), or over spoon handle. In this way, you throw a fine thread of sugar. When there is a good quantity of threads on rolling pin or spoon handle, draw them off carefully and hang on a hook, eg. a dresser hook. When ready for use, carefully lift them off, fold them lightly and set threads over the sweet to be decorated.

Watchpoint You must leave syrup for about 1 minute before starting to spin it and only dip the forks just into the syrup. If syrup is too thin, or there's too much on forks, you'll get drops among the threads.

Pineapple Ninon

1 ripe pineapple
selection of the following fruit :
   orange sections, green grapes,
   whole glacé cherries, lychees,
   sliced pears, strawberries, bananas
sugar (for dusting)
2 tablespoons kirsch
about $\frac{1}{4}$ pint double cream

For almond pastry
2 oz plain flour
pinch of salt
1 oz ground almonds
1 oz butter
1 oz caster sugar
1 egg yolk

6-8 small fluted, or plain, tartlet tins

Method

To prepare the pastry : make it up as for French flan pastry (see method page 154), sprinkling the almonds on the flour. Chill, then roll out and line into the tins. Bake blind. Take out of the tins and leave until cool.

Use a serrated knife to cut the top off the pineapple, then cut flesh out of the skin. Lift the pineapple flesh into a dish, slice and core. Prepare the chosen fruit and put in the dish with the pineapple; dust with sugar and sprinkle with kirsch. Cover and leave for about 1 hour in the coldest part of the refrigerator.

When ready to serve take a flat silver, or steel, dish and arrange the hollowed-out pineapple on this and fill with the fruit. Surround with the little tartlets filled with whipped cream. If wished, a veil of spun sugar (see page 38) could be thrown over the top of the pineapple.

Tartlets filled with whipped cream accompany the pineapple Ninon

Pineapple flambé 1

1 pineapple
caster sugar (for dusting)
4-6 slices of stale sponge cake
about 3 oz butter
2 fl oz brandy, or rum

Chafing dish or flameproof pan

Method
Slice the peel from the pineapple, cut into slices and core. Dust well with caster sugar and set aside. Heat the chafing dish, brown the slices of sponge cake in about 1 oz butter until a light brown, dusting lightly with caster sugar during the frying time. Arrange cake on a hot dish. Wipe out the pan, drop in 1-2 oz butter, put in the slices of pineapple, dust well with sugar and cook rapidly until just beginning to colour. Turn on full heat, pour in the brandy and dish up on the sponge cake while still flaming.

Pineapple flambé 2

1 pineapple (peeled, cored, sliced and lightly sugared)
2-4 tablespoons kirsch
2-4 tablespoons brandy
caster sugar (for dusting)

Chafing dish or flameproof pan

Method
Lay the pineapple in the chafing dish and sprinkle with kirsch. Set on a moderate flame and shake the pan until hot, giving a further sprinkling of kirsch. When it is just hot, shake in a dusting of sugar and then give a really good sprinkling of brandy. Shake pan well, allowing the liquid to catch alight. Serve while still flaming.

Flambé dishes can be prepared in the dining room if you have a chafing dish or flameproof pan and a burner

Gooseberry fool

2 lb gooseberries
½-¾ pint water
3-4 elderflower heads
caster sugar (to taste)
½ pint double cream
sponge fingers, or crisp biscuits

For thick custard
1 dessertspoon custard powder,
   or 3 egg yolks and 1 teaspoon
   arrowroot
¼ pint milk

Method
Top and tail and wash the gooseberries, put them into a pan with the water. Tie the elderflowers in a small piece of muslin, add this to the pan and cover it. Simmer until the fruit is soft, then take out the elder-flowers, drain off juice, reserve.

To make custard : cream egg yolks and arrowroot in a bowl, heat milk to just below boiling point and pour on gradually. Blend and strain back into unused pan. Stir gently over low heat until mixture thickens. If using custard powder, follow instructions on packet. Set aside to cool.

Rub the fruit through a nylon sieve or pass through a fine Mouli sieve. Measure this purée, which should be about 1 pint (make up with juice, if not), sweeten to taste and, when quite cold, mix with the custard. Half whip the cream and fold it into the custard mixture, leaving the fool slightly 'marbled' with the cream. Serve in glasses or in a bowl, with sponge fingers or crisp biscuits.

Plum suédoise

1½ lb red plums (stoned—see page 15)
sugar syrup (made with ½ pint water,
   and 4 rounded tablespoons
   granulated sugar — see page 15)
scant ¾ oz gelatine
a few almonds (blanched) — see
   page 154

6-inch diameter deep cake tin, or charlotte tin (1½ pints capacity)

Method
Make the sugar syrup, then halve plums and poach them in it, making sure that they cook for at least 15 minutes to develop the flavour. Drain the fruit and keep a few of the best halves on one side ; reserve syrup. Rub remaining halves through a nylon strainer into a bowl.

Measure $\frac{3}{4}$ pint of the syrup and pour $\frac{1}{2}$ pint into the fruit purée. Soak and dissolve the gelatine over heat in the remaining $\frac{1}{4}$ pint of syrup and mix with purée. Put half a blanched almond in each reserved plum half and arrange at the bottom of wet tin, cut sides to the base of the tin.

When purée is on point of setting, carefully pour into wet tin ; leave in a cool place to set.

Turn out and serve with whipped fresh cream.

Plum Condé

1 lb plums (stoned — see page 15)
sugar syrup (made with ½ pint water
    and 3 tablespoons granulated
    sugar — see page 15)
3 tablespoons Carolina rice
1 pint milk
1 tablespoon granulated sugar
2-3 drops of vanilla essence
scant ½ oz gelatine
1 tablespoon cold water
3½ fl oz double cream
1 egg white

Savarin mould (lightly oiled)

Method
Make sugar syrup, halve plums
and poach them in it until
tender. Allow to get quite cold.
Meanwhile wash the rice in a
nylon or fine wire strainer held
under cold tap, and drain well.

Bring milk to boil, add rice
and cook gently until tender;
stir occasionally to prevent
sticking. Test the rice after
25-30 minutes and when absolutely tender and nearly all milk
has been absorbed remove from
the heat. Add sugar and vanilla
essence and turn rice mixture
into a basin to cool.

Soak the gelatine in 1 tablespoon of cold water, then add
5 tablespoons of the plum
syrup; melt the gelatine over
gentle heat and add carefully to
the rice. Whip the cream lightly
and whisk the egg white until
stiff, then fold them both into
the rice cream. Pour the mixture
into the savarin mould, cover
with foil and leave in a cool
place to set. Drain the plums.

When set, turn rice cream on
to serving dish, arrange plums
overlapping in centre. Rub any
remaining plums through a
nylon strainer and dilute with
some syrup to make a sauce.

Peasant girl in a veil

2 lb ripe red plums
4 oz granulated sugar
8 tablespoons white breadcrumbs
2 oz butter
a little caster sugar
¼ pint double cream
1 egg white

Method
Set oven at 350°F or Mark 4.

Wipe the plums, split and
remove stones (see page 15).
Lay plums in an ovenproof
dish and sprinkle thickly with
sugar, cover and cook in pre-
set moderate oven for 35-40
minutes until soft. Allow to cool.

Fry the crumbs in butter until
brown, scattering with a little
caster sugar. Lay the plums, free
from juice, in a glass dish or
bowl in layers with the crumbs.
Whisk the cream until partially
whipped. Whisk egg white until
it stands in peaks and fold into
the cream. Spread over plums
and chill before serving.

Plum compote
with rich almond cake

1 lb red plums
1 wineglass red wine, or port
4 tablespoons redcurrant jelly
(see page 155)
grated rind and juice of 1 orange

Method
Pour wine into a pan large enough to take the plums, boil until reduced to half the quantity. Add redcurrant jelly, stir gently until dissolved, then add the orange rind and juice.

Halve and stone the plums (see page 15) and put rounded side down (cut side uppermost) in the pan; let syrup boil up and over fruit, then poach gently until fruit is quite tender. Allow a full 10 minutes for this, even if the fruit is ripe.

Turn fruit into a bowl to cool; serve with a rich almond cake (see right).

Rich almond cake
4 oz butter
5 oz caster sugar
3 eggs
3 oz ground almonds
1½ oz plain flour
2-3 drops of almond essence

Deep 7-inch diameter sandwich tin

Method
Grease and flour sandwich tin, cover base with disc of greaseproof paper; set the oven at 350°F or Mark 4.

Soften butter with a wooden spoon in a bowl, add the sugar a tablespoon at a time, and beat thoroughly until mixture is soft and light. Add the eggs, one at a time, adding one-third of the almonds with each egg. Beat well. Fold in the flour and almond essence with a metal spoon and turn cake mixture into the prepared tin.

Bake in pre-set oven for 45-50 minutes until cake is cooked. (Test by inserting a thin skewer; it should come out clean.) When cooked, the cake should also shrink very slightly from the sides of the tin.

To turn out, have ready two wire cooling racks, put a clean folded tea towel or single thickness of absorbent paper on one of them. Loosen the sides of the cake with a round-bladed knife, place the rack with the towel or paper on top of the cake (towel next to it) and turn over; remove the tin and disc of paper from the base.

Place second rack on top of cake base and carefully and quickly turn it over again. This prevents the rack marking top of cake. Dust top with caster sugar.

Raw ingredients for plum compote

Rhubarb fool

1 lb rhubarb
sugar syrup (made with ¼ pint water
   and 2 tablespoons granulated
   sugar — see page 15)
1 tablespoon caster sugar
¼ pint thick custard (made with ¼ pint
   milk and 3 egg yolks, or
   1 dessertspoon custard powder
   to ¼ pint milk)
¼ pint double cream

To serve
sponge fingers, or crisp biscuits

Method
Make sugar syrup. Prepare the
rhubarb (see page 15) and cook
in the syrup. Drain and rub
through a strainer into a bowl.
Sweeten to taste with caster
sugar and set aside to cool.

To prepare the custard; beat
egg yolks in bowl; gently heat
milk in a pan (do not boil).
Pour on to egg yolks and mix.
Strain back into rinsed pan.
Stir gently over low heat until
mixture thickens (about 15
minutes), set aside to cool. If
using custard powder, follow
instructions on packet.

When the custard is cold mix
into the purée. Whip the cream
lightly and fold into the rhubarb
mixture, leaving it with a
marbled effect.

Serve in glasses or in a bowl,
with a few sponge fingers or
crisp biscuits handed separately.

Mrs Rudge. 6.30.

Chatham. 65293.

Mrs Flannery. 9.30 pm.
Mrs Parker 10.00 am

For Anneke.

Carlisle - Halber.

Mrs Roberts. 33, Association Walk.
Warner Ward.
Rochester.

3.30.
73, Riverside Rd
on Sun hr.

Con

43 of Sl... p...
K.J.H.

Fresh fruit salad with almond biscuits

(For photograph of finished dish, see page 9)

2 oranges
2 clementines
3 ripe pears
8 oz grapes
3 bananas
2-3 tablespoons liqueur (kirsch, or maraschino) — optional
sugar syrup (made with 6 table-spoons water, 3 oz granulated sugar and strip of lemon rind, or piece of vanilla pod)

Method

First prepare the sugar syrup : dissolve sugar slowly in the water, add lemon rind or vanilla pod, and boil for 1 minute. Tip into a bowl and leave to cool. Remove flavouring.

Cut peel, pith and first skin from oranges with a sharp, serrated-edge knife to expose flesh ; then remove segments by cutting between each membrane. Peel and slice clementines. Peel and quarter pears, remove core, cut each quarter into two. Pip grapes by hooking out pips with eye of a trussing needle. Only white grapes should be peeled, not black ones. If skin is difficult to remove from white grapes, dip them into boiling water for 1 minute. Peel bananas and cut in thick, slanting slices.

Moisten fruit with sugar syrup, add liqueur and turn fruit over carefully. Set a plate on top to keep fruit covered by the syrup. Chill before serving.

Almond biscuits

3 oz butter
3 oz caster sugar
2 oz plain flour
pinch of salt
3 oz almonds (finely shredded)

These biscuits are known as 'tuiles' because they resemble curved tiles.

Method

First, set the oven at 400°F or Mark 6. Soften butter, add sugar and beat well with wooden spoon until light and fluffy. Sift flour with a pinch of salt and stir into the mixture with the almonds. Put mixture a teaspoon at a time on to a well-greased baking tin and flatten with a wet fork.

Watchpoint Leave plenty of space between the biscuits because they will spread during cooking.

Bake in the oven until just coloured (6-8 minutes). Allow to stand a second or two before removing from the tin with a sharp knife. Curl on a rolling pin until set. Store when cool in an airtight container.

Curling the cooked almond biscuits or tuiles can be tricky ; if they are allowed to get too cool, they will break when you try to mould them

Apple chartreuse

1 large cooking apple
½ pint water
8 oz lump sugar
pared rind and strained juice of
   1 lemon
2 lb crisp dessert apples (Cox's
   Orange Pippin, or Russet, or
   Sturmer)
4 oz candied fruit (mixture of
   glacé cherry, angelica,
   pineapple, apricot and
   orange peel) — chopped

6-inch diameter cake tin (1¼ pints
*   capacity), or 6-inch diameter top*
*   (No. 2 size) soufflé dish*

Tipping the cooked apples and
candied fruits into soufflé dish to set

Method

Wipe the cooking apple, remove the stalk and eye, cut in slices but do not remove the peel, core or pips. Put slices in a saucepan with the water, cover and simmer gently until pulpy. Tip into a nylon strainer, over a bowl, and leave undisturbed until all the juice has dripped through. Measure the amount of juice (you need $7\frac{1}{2}$ fl oz) and put this in a large shallow pan with the sugar, rind and lemon juice and set on a low heat. When all the sugar has dissolved, boil juice steadily for 5 minutes, draw pan aside and remove the lemon rind.

Peel and core the dessert apples and slice straight into the pan of juice — they must be cut very evenly and quite thinly ($\frac{1}{8}$ inch). Cover the pan and cook apples gently for 10-12 minutes. **Watchpoint** During this cooking time turn the apple slices once or twice, taking great care not to break them or let the syrup boil — it should just simmer very gently.

Take the lid off the pan and continue cooking until there is just enough syrup to moisten the apple slices. Draw off the heat, add the candied fruits, cover the pan and leave until the apples look clear. Tip into the wet cake tin or soufflé dish and leave in a cool place to set. (No gelatine is needed with this chartreuse as the natural pectin in the fruit is sufficient to set it.)

Turn chartreuse out of the tin or dish and serve with fresh cream or soured cream sauce, or a sharp rum and apricot sauce (see right). We think the slightly sharp flavour of soured cream goes particularly well with this pudding.

Rum and apricot sauce

4 tablespoons smooth apricot jam
2 tablespoons water
juice of $\frac{1}{2}$ lemon
1 tablespoon rum

Method

Put jam, water and the lemon juice in a pan and heat gently to melt the jam. Bring sauce to the boil. Remove from the heat, add rum and strain sauce into a bowl. Serve cold.

Soured cream sauce

$\frac{1}{4}$ pint double cream
$\frac{1}{4}$ pint soured cream
1 teaspoon caster sugar

Method

Whip double cream, until it begins to thicken, then stir in the soured cream and caster sugar.

Chartreuse of golden fruit

1 can (15oz) Cape golden
  berries
1 can (11 oz) mandarin oranges
2 ripe Hale peaches
2 pints liquid lemon jelly (see page
  72)
lightly whipped cream (optional)

Ring mould (2½-2¾ pints capacity)

Method
First drain the canned fruits thoroughly. Scald and peel the peaches, then slice them. Pour enough jelly into the mould to cover the bottom to a depth of a bare ½ inch.

Put in a layer of the golden berries and set with more cool jelly, then a layer of the mandarin oranges, set again with the jelly, then put in a layer of peaches and set with jelly. Continue in this way until the mould is full. The last layer should be of jelly. Leave to set (preferably overnight).

To serve, dip the mould into warm water, then turn out and if wished fill the centre with lightly whipped cream or chopped jelly. If filling with chopped jelly, cream could be served separately.

Macedoine of tropical fruits

1 can of mangoes
1 small can of lychees
3 oranges

This would be made from fresh fruits in the tropics but in Britain you can use canned fruit with fresh oranges.

Method
Tip the mangoes into a crystal bowl, drain the lychees and put in with the mangoes. Peel the oranges and cut in sections or slices, as preferred, and mix carefully with the other fruit. Cover and chill before serving.

Fruits rafraîchis

selection of fresh fruit (1-1½ lb)
4-5 tablespoons thick syrup
  (made with 6 oz caster sugar
  and 6 fl oz water see page 15)
3-4 tablespoons kirsch (optional)

Method
Prepare the fruit and place it in a glass bowl or dish. Spoon over a small quantity of syrup. Flavour with a little kirsch if wished. Cover and chill for 2-3 hours until wanted. Serve separately in a glass bowl.

Ices and iced puddings

A hot summer day calls for a cold iced pudding. Home-made ices and iced puddings are a sure recipe for success when the weather is hot and humid. Children come in from play thirsty and sticky; guests are too hot to eat unless you tempt them with promises of cool relief; the most acceptable choice is an ice.

Home-made cream and water ices are completely different in both flavour and texture from commercially prepared varieties. Many people appreciate this and are more than willing to give that little extra time and trouble to making them, and to invest in a special machine.

Though cream and water ices can be made in the ice cube trays of the refrigerator (minus the cube divisions) they haven't the quality or velvety texture of one that is made in a machine, where the mixture is churned or beaten continually while freezing. To be really good, ices should be made an hour or more before serving and left in the tray or container. Alternatively they can be moulded and deep-frozen.

Sugar content in ices
The amount of sugar in the mixture to be frozen is important — whether for a cream or water ice. Too sweet a mixture will not freeze; one not sweet enough gives a hard and tasteless ice. Though to a certain extent this can be corrected once the mixture is made, it is wise to start working to a definite proportion (as given in the basic recipes).

The proportion of sugar is even more important in a water ice than a cream one to give the right soft, yet firm, consistency. It helps to test by tasting, but keep on the sweet side, especially if there is a fruit base, eg. raspberry, blackcurrant or pineapple. The flavour is weakened by freezing, so always taste the mixture before pouring it into the container.

Methods of freezing
In refrigerator or home-freezer. Use the ice trays of a refrigerator or a stainless steel bowl in a home-freezer. In both these cases, the mixture must be well stirred about every hour and, as it thickens, stirred and beaten

51

more frequently until it barely holds its shape. Then smooth over the top and cover with foil. Leave for at least an hour to 'ripen' before serving.

For freezing a water ice in the refrigerator, see lemon water ice (basic recipe) on page 54.

Churn freezer. This type can be manual or electric. The former is more generally used, and it consists of a wooden bucket with a metal container fitted with a dasher. The bucket is first packed with a combination of ice and salt, and the ice-cream mixture is poured into the container. A handle is then turned which revolves the dasher, and so not only gradually scrapes away the mixture from round the sides as it freezes, but also churns, or beats, it at the same time.

The electric churn machines, of which there are two types, operate on the same principle. One type is set in the ice-making compartment of the refrigerator (so that there is no necessity for extra ice), with the flex leading to an electric plug outside the refrigerator. The other variety requires a quantity of ice.

The mixture to be frozen must not come more than half to three-quarters of the way up the sides of the container. This allows for what is called 'swell', ie. when the cream mixture is churned the quantity increases and rises in the container. A water ice has slightly less swell, and it is not apparent until the egg white has been added (see lemon water ice).

To obtain a low freezing temperature a mixture of ice and salt is used. The salt should be coarse rock salt (known as freezing salt), obtainable from some fishmongers and from big stores. The ice is best chipped off from a block rather than ice made by an ice-maker. The latter is in pellets (or small cubes), which are uneconomical as churn freezers require constant refilling. Being small, the pellets melt very quickly. As they are usually square, they do not, therefore, fit well around the machine.

Unfortunately, with the wider use of refrigerators and home-freezers, many fishmongers only stock ice made by an ice-maker. Those who are fortunate enough to possess a roomy home-freezer can freeze water in any suitable container, break or chip it into convenient-sized pieces, then store it in polythene bags for future use.

To chip ice, use an ice pick consisting of a single spike fitted into a wooden handle. To break the ice, put the block on several layers of newspaper on the floor or, if more convenient, in the sink. Give short sharp jabs at the piece or block of ice with the pick ; avoid going right through down to the paper.

Watchpoint The pieces of ice should not be so large that the salt trickles through the gaps between them, as would certainly happen if ice cubes from the refrigerator were used. This can be prevented if the pieces are well jabbed down when filling them into the bucket.

How to churn
Start by turning the handle smoothly and evenly for about 3 minutes. Then leave for a further 3-4 minutes. Test the handle again, and if it shows any resistance continue to churn until the handle is really stiff to turn round. If the mixture is made with the right proportion of sugar, the time for

churning should not exceed 5-6 minutes.

In the early stages, a cream mixture can be left in the container longer than 3 minutes, and water ices up to 5 minutes. This allows the mixture to get really cold and therefore shortens the time of churning. During this period, test the handle every minute or so and, as soon as resistance is felt, start at once to churn regularly. Keep the bucket topped up with ice and salt, if necessary, but do this during the initial period, before the main churning.

When ice is really stiff, stop churning and pour off any water from the hole in the side of the bucket. Wipe lid free of any water or salt, then remove the centre bar and lid carefully and lift up dasher with one hand, holding the container down with the other. Scrape the dasher free from mixture with a plastic scraper or table knife. Push mixture down from around the sides into the bottom of the container.

Cover the top with a piece of foil, or double sheet of greaseproof paper, and replace the lid. Bung the hole in the lid with a screw of paper and fill up the bucket with more ice and salt. Cover the top with a thick cloth; use a floor or oven cloth or a piece of sacking. Set the churn in a cool place and leave for 1 hour or longer. If left for longer than 1 hour, however, the melted ice will have to be drained off and the bucket replenished with ice.

Watchpoint It is important to avoid the handle getting stuck, ie. this occurs if the mixture has been left too long in the packed machine during the first stage or if the later churning has been interrupted.

Too much pressure put on the handle results in damaging the cogs in the ratchet and possibly breaking the wooden flanges of the dasher. It is equally important to avoid any grain of salt or salty water getting into the mixture, hence the necessity to wipe the lid clean before removing it.

Serving the finished ice
Whether making cream or water ices, it is wise to invest in an ice scoop. This makes the job easier and also gives an indication as to how much ice-cream to make. These scoops are numbered on the handle, 18-20 etc., indicating the number of scoops obtainable from 1 quart of ice-cream.

To serve, have a jug of cold water ready alongside the container, dip the scoop in the water and then into the ice mixture. When full, level off the scoop with a knife or against the side of the container. Hold it over the dish or coupe glass and press the spring on the handle which releases the ice mixture. Then dip the scoop into the water and repeat the process.

Water ice

A water ice is essentially a fruit-flavoured, light syrup, either lemon or orange, or a fruit purée with syrup added. This type is best churned in a freezer, but it can be made in a refrigerator if a small quantity of gelatine is added.

Water ice is frozen to a slush before a very small quantity of egg white, whipped to a firm snow, is added and the freezing is continued until the ice is firm. The addition of egg white binds the ice together and makes for a smooth, yet firm, consistency.

The recipe for lemon water ice (right) gives the basic method.

The term 'sorbet' originally referred to a Turkish iced drink. Today, bought water ices are often called sorbets, probably because the name is more attractive commercially.

A true sorbet has a lemon or orange water ice base flavoured with liqueur, with Italian meringue added. A sorbet used to be served between the entrée and roast during a long menu to refresh the palate.

Adding a little whipped egg white to churn when making water ice

Lemon water ice

1¼ pints water
pared rind and juice of 3 large and juicy lemons
7 oz lump sugar
½ egg white (whisked)
scant ½ oz gelatine

Method
Put the water, lemon rind and sugar into a scrupulously clean pan, bring slowly to the boil, simmer for 5 minutes, then strain into a jug. Strain the lemon juice and add to jug, mix well and taste for sweetness. Chill well before freezing.

Pour mixture into the packed freezer, leave for 5 minutes, then churn to a slush. Whip egg white to a firm snow and add ¾-1 tablespoon to ice. Churn it until firm. Remove dasher and pack down.
Note : if freezing the ice in a refrigerator, dissolve the gelatine in a small quantity of the sugar syrup after straining. Add to the jug with the lemon juice. Chill before pouring into ice trays. Turn refrigerator down to the maximum freezing temperature, freeze to a slush, then beat in the required amount of egg white. Return to the ice compartment, freeze until just firm, then beat again, cover with foil and return to the ice compartment. Turn refrigerator back to normal and leave the ice until required.
Watchpoint The quantity of egg white varies according to consistency desired for individual recipes. Half a white is the smallest quantity it is possible to whisk, but it may not be necessary to use it all.

Orange water ice

4 large oranges
pared rind and juice of 2 lemons
8 oz lump sugar
1½ pints water
½ egg white (whisked)

Method
Put the rind of the lemon into a pan with 6 oz sugar and the water and dissolve over heat. Draw pan aside, then rub the remaining lumps of sugar on to the rind of the oranges to remove the zest. Do this thoroughly. Return the pan to the heat and boil mixture for a further 5 minutes, then draw pan aside, add the lumps of sugar, allow them to dissolve and return pan to heat for about 30 seconds. Remove pan from heat, add the strained juice of the lemons and oranges to the mixture and chill.

Pour mixture into a churn freezer and churn as directed in the general instructions. Add ¾-1 tablespoon of the egg white, whisked to a firm snow, when the ice is frozen to a slush. Continue to churn until firm then pack down. The ice is now ready to serve.

Blackcurrant leaf water ice

4 large handfuls of blackcurrant
    leaves (washed)
pared rind and juice of 3 large
    lemons
7 oz lump sugar
1½ pints water
2-3 drops of edible green colouring
½ egg white (whisked)

The infusion of blackcurrant leaves gives the ice a strong flavour of muscat grapes.

Method
Put the rind into a pan with the sugar and the water. Dissolve sugar completely, then boil rapidly for 5 minutes and add the washed blackcurrant leaves. Cover the pan and draw off the heat. Allow liquid to infuse until well flavoured, then strain, squeezing the leaves well to extract all the syrup. Add the strained lemon juice and the colouring.

Freeze mixture and, when it is a slush, add 1 dessertspoon of egg white, whisked to a firm snow. Stir in, or churn, remaining egg white, then continue to freeze until firm. Serve plain or with sugared fruit, or with Charentais melon.

Raspberry water ice

2 lb raspberries
2-3 tablespoons icing sugar
$\frac{1}{2}$ egg white (whisked)
sugar syrup (made from 7 fl oz
    water and 6 oz granulated sugar)

Method

Make the sugar syrup by dissolving sugar in the water over gentle heat, then boiling for 3-4 minutes. Leave this syrup to get cold.

Purée the raspberries by either rubbing them through a nylon sieve or putting them in a blender. If using a blender, strain the purée to get rid of any pieces of seed. Add about 2-3 tablespoons icing sugar to purée to sweeten it lightly.

Gradually add the cold sugar syrup to the purée, stirring well. Taste for sweetness, then chill. Turn ice into a churn freezer and churn until it forms a slush. Then whisk the egg white and add 1 tablespoon of this to the mixture. Continue to churn the ice, and when it is really firm remove dasher and pack down. **Note :** 1 lb of juicy raspberries should yield about 7-8 fl oz, thus 2 lb should make just under 1 pint. If a little short on quantity, extra syrup can be added ; do this while making the raspberries into a purée, rinsing off the purée from the sieve or the sides of the blender with the sugar syrup. Taste for strength of flavour and sweetness.

Pineapple water ice

1 large pineapple
soft fruit (eg. raspberries,
    strawberries, or currants)

For ice
6 oz lump sugar
1 pint water
pared rind and juice of 1 large
    lemon
$\frac{1}{2}$ egg white (whisked)

To garnish
vine, or strawberry, leaves

Method

Dissolve the sugar in the water with the pared rind of the lemon and boil for 4-5 minutes ; then add the lemon juice, strain, and leave liquid to cool.

Split the pineapple in two, lengthways, and slice out the pulp with a grapefruit knife, removing the large centre core. With a fork break the flesh of the pineapple into shreds and measure this. There should be $\frac{3}{4}$-1 pint. Add this pulp to the cold syrup and freeze as for lemon water ice (page 54), adding 1 tablespoon whisked egg white when it forms a slush.

Chill the pineapple halves and, when ready to serve, put the fresh soft fruit in the bottom of the pineapple halves and set the ice on top. Arrange the pineapple halves on a silver dish lined with green leaves, such as vine leaves or strawberry leaves.

Cream ices

Cream ices are made on a base of either egg mousse or custard, with a proportion of egg white added. When the mousse or custard is cold, cream is folded into the mixture.

For cream ices made on an egg mousse base, single cream can be used. If using double cream, partially whip it to give the ice a smoother and richer consistency.

As with water ices, freezing diminishes the flavour and colour of cream ices, so this must always be taken into consideration when tasting the unfrozen mixture.

Vanilla cream ice 1

2 eggs
2 egg yolks
3 oz caster sugar
1 pint milk
1 vanilla pod, or 2-3 drops of
   vanilla essence
¼ pint single cream, or double
   cream (lightly whipped)

This is the basic method for making cream ices on a custard base.

The caster sugar may be flavoured with a vanilla pod. This is done by leaving a dry pod in a small jar of caster sugar for a few days. The vanilla in the recipe may then be omitted.

Method
Break the whole eggs into a bowl, add the separated egg yolks, then the sugar and whisk to mix well, but not so that the mixture becomes slushy.

Scald the milk (if using a vanilla pod, split it and add to the milk). When it is at boiling point, remove vanilla pod and pour milk on the egg mixture, stirring vigorously. Strain custard and allow to cool. If using vanilla essence, add it at this point.

When custard is quite cold, add the cream, then freeze it in the refrigerator ice tray, or in a churn freezer.

Vanilla cream ice 2

1 vanilla pod, or 2-3 drops vanilla
   essence
1¼ pints single, or double, cream
3 oz granulated sugar
4 fl oz water
4 egg yolks (well beaten)

This ice is made on an egg mousse base, and is thus more suitable for making in a refrigerator than Vanilla cream ice 1.

Method
Split the vanilla pod and scoop out a few seeds. Put the cream into a pan with the vanilla pod (but if using essence, do not add at this stage). Leave it to infuse, covered, for about 7-10 minutes on a low heat until cream is well scalded, ie. just below simmering point. Strain cream, cover with greaseproof paper to prevent a skin forming and leave to cool.

Put the sugar and the water into a small pan, stir over gentle heat until the sugar is dissolved, then boil steadily without shaking or stirring until the syrup reaches the 'thread' stage (when a little **cooled** syrup will form a thread between finger and thumb).

Have the egg yolks ready, then draw pan of syrup aside and, when the bubbles have subsided, pour it on to the yolks and whisk well with a rotary whisk until mixture is thick and mousse-like. Add the cream (and vanilla essence, if used) and mix well. Chill mixture thoroughly before freezing it.

Chocolate cream ice

7 oz plain block chocolate
2 oz granulated sugar
4 fl oz water
3 egg yolks (well beaten)
vanilla essence, rum or brandy
   (to flavour) — optional
1¼ pints single cream

A chocolate cream ice is usually flavoured with vanilla, unless rum or brandy is added.

Method
Put sugar and water into a pan, dissolve sugar over gentle heat, then boil steadily until the syrup reaches the 'thread' stage (see left). Have the well-beaten yolks ready, carefully pour syrup on to them, whisk to a thick mousse-like mixture, add flavouring; then set aside.

Break up the chocolate, put into a pan with the cream and dissolve slowly over gentle heat. Bring it to scalding point, then draw pan aside and allow to cool, then add to mousse. Chill mixture before freezing.
Note : if wished, half single and half double cream may be used. In this case dissolve the chocolate in the single cream and, when added to the egg mousse, lightly whip the double cream and add this to the mixture, then freeze.

> **Chocolate cream ice** can also be made using the vanilla cream ice 1 recipe (see left). Take the same quantity of chocolate as above, dissolve in the milk, then add mixture to egg yolks.

Brown bread cream ice

vanilla cream ice 2 (see far left)
about ¾ stale loaf of brown bread
caster sugar
Melba sauce (see page 28)

Method
Remove crusts from bread and make bread into crumbs. Sprinkle with caster sugar and toast crumbs until a good brown in a hot oven at 375°F or Mark 5. This should make 6 tablespoons. Leave to get cold.

Churn the vanilla cream ice until almost set, then quickly add the crumbs and continue to churn for 1-2 minutes. Pack down and leave to ripen.

Serve ice on a chilled dish with the sauce of your choice.

Plum pudding ice

2 oz currants
4 oz stoned raisins
½ oz blanched almonds
½ oz candied orange peel
1 oz glacé cherries
½ wineglass brandy, or rum

For cream ice mixture
6 oz plain block chocolate, or 2 oz
   cocoa and 2½ fl oz cold water
1 pint single, or ½ pint single and
   ½ pint double, cream
2 oz granulated sugar
2½ fl oz water
3 egg yolks

To decorate
whipped double cream (flavoured
   with brandy, or rum)

*Plum pudding ice decorated with a
ruff of flavoured, whipped cream*

Method
First prepare the fruit. Wash the currants and raisins well, finely shred the almonds and candied orange peel and rinse the cherries to get rid of some of the heavy syrup. Pour over the brandy (or rum) and leave fruit to macerate for 1-2 hours.

To prepare the cream ice mixture: dissolve chocolate in the single cream over gentle heat. If using cocoa, mix with the cold water and cook to a thick cream, then add this to the single cream and scald.

Make an egg mousse with the sugar, water and yolks (see Vanilla cream ice 2 — page 58) and add to the cream; if using double cream as well, whip it lightly and add to the mousse mixture. Chill in the refrigerator.

When the mixture is chilled, turn it into a churn freezer and churn until very thick. Then add the fruit and continue to churn until really firm. Remove the dasher and pack down.

Serve cream ice on a chilled serving dish scooped out in the form of a plum pudding. Decorate, if wished, with a ruff of whipped cream, flavoured with brandy (or rum).

Fruit cream ice

1 pint fruit purée (lightly
  sweetened)
4 oz granulated sugar
scant ¼ pint water
3 egg yolks (well beaten)
¾ pint single cream

The fruit purée may be made
with raspberries, apricots or
blackcurrants, etc., and if using
a strong-flavoured fruit, such
as blackcurrants or damsons,
add more sugar than you would
to, say, a strawberry purée.

Method
For the fruit purée : damsons
and other firm fruit such as
gooseberries or apricots should
be first cooked and then made
into a purée. Soft fruit, such as
raspberries and strawberries,
can be made into a purée when
raw. To purée, either rub
through a nylon sieve or work
in a blender ; if using a blender,
strain this purée before use.
Prepare an egg mousse with
the sugar, water and yolks as
for Vanilla cream ice 2 (see page
58). When cool, add the cream
and purée. Taste to make sure
that it is sufficiently sweet.
Freeze in the ice compartment
of refrigerator, or in a churn
freezer.

Glace en surprise

strawberry, raspberry, or chocolate
  cream ice (see left and page 59)

For sponge
3 oz plain flour
pinch of salt
2 eggs
4 oz caster sugar

For meringue
2 egg whites
4 oz caster sugar
2-3 drops of vanilla essence
caster sugar (for dusting)

*8-inch diameter sandwich tin ;
forcing bag with 8- or 10-cut rose
pipe*

Method
Prepare sponge cake (see method
Gâteau Margot, page 118), and
bake in moderate oven for 20-30
minutes until risen and brown.
Turn out and cool on rack.
Choose a plated or silver dish
and chill it well. Half fill a large
roasting tin with ice and freezing
salt and set the dish in this.
Set the oven at 350°F or Mark
4. To prepare meringue : whisk
the egg whites stiffly, add 2-3
rounded teaspoons of the caster
sugar and vanilla essence and
whisk again until stiff. Fold in
the remaining sugar. Fill into
the forcing bag.
Place the sponge cake on the
dish, scoop out the cream ice
and arrange on top of the
sponge. Pipe the meringue over
the ice to cover it completely.
Dust the meringue well with
caster sugar ; leave for 1 minute,
then put the cake into pre-set
moderate oven. Cook for about
4 minutes or until the meringue
is lightly browned. Serve at once.

Iced puddings

Bombes are so called because of their bomb-shape moulds, which are made of tin-lined copper with a screw at the base and a tight-fitting lid. These were so designed for easy burying in a mixture of ice and salt, but nowadays a refrigerator with a large ice-making compartment, or preferably a home-freezer, is used. This means that no lid is necessary provided that the top is well covered with foil. Unless the special bombe shape is wanted, the ices in these recipes can be frozen in a cake tin or spring-form tin.

For this type of pudding the ice mixture must first be frozen until really firm, then filled to the brim in the previously chilled mould. If using a bombe mould, grease the edge with lard, cover with greaseproof paper and the lid; if using a cake tin just cover with foil.

For freezing a bombe in the ice-making compartment of the refrigerator, turn the temperature down to maximum cold; do this 30 minutes before putting in the mould. Leave the mould in the refrigerator for 4 hours or longer. If freezing it in a home-freezer, 2-3 hours should be long enough.

If you only have a small ice-making compartment in your refrigerator which will not take a mould, and no home-freezer, use a large pail with ice and salt in the same proportion as for the churn freezer (see page 52). But the mould used must be a bombe, or at least one with a tight-fitting lid. Smear around the edge of the mould with lard, and, if using a bombe, make sure that the screw is tight before burying the mould in ice and salt. Cover the pail with a thick cloth, or piece of blanket, and leave in a

To seal a bombe mould: smear the edge with lard, cover first with greaseproof paper, then lid

To bury bombe mould: place in a pail of ice and freezing salt, making sure it is well covered

cool place for 3-4 hours. Tip off any water when necessary and refill with ice.

To turn out the bombe. If frozen in ice and salt, draw the mould through a large bowl of cold water. Dry and remove lid, replace it, but not tightly, and draw again through a bowl of fresh cold water. Two 'swishings' through the water should be enough. This not only loosens the ice in the mould or tin, but also washes away the salt. Dry again and remove the lid and paper.

Have the serving dish ready; it is best to use a well-chilled silver or stainless steel one. Turn the bombe over and unscrew the knob at the base which should release the suction and so cause the ice to drop on to the dish. If bombe does not slide out, wrap a hot cloth around mould or keep your hands on it for about 30 seconds. Draw the mould off gently. Finish the ice with a ruff of cream piped round the base, or pour round a cold sauce : eg Melba or chocolate (see pages 28 and 153).

To turn out ices set in cake tins and spring-form tins : turn out in the same way as for bombes, but draw them 2-3 times through a bowl of cold water. Dry as before, remove foil, then turn out and decorate.

If you feel ambitious, you may use two differently flavoured ices : one to clothe, or line, the inside of the mould by about 1 inch, the other to fill the centre. Alternatively the centre can be filled with lightly

To turn out the bombe mould first release the knob at the base

whipped, sweetened cream. For example, coffee cream ice outside, whipped cream, mixed with sliced ginger, or chocolate caraque (see page 153), inside.

Parfait. This second type of iced pudding is a delicate and rich sweet, made with a rich mousse base and lightly whipped cream. It is flavoured according to the recipe. The mixture is not frozen first, but is turned directly into a mould, either a bombe or a cake tin, well covered and deep frozen, as for a bombe, for 3-4 hours. When turned out, a parfait should just hold its shape.

Bombe Diane

3 tablespoons instant coffee
   powder
$\frac{1}{2}$ pint single cream
1 egg
2 egg yolks
2 oz caster sugar
$\frac{1}{2}$ pint double cream

For filling
4-5 bananas
1 tablespoon lemon juice, or rum
little icing sugar
$\frac{1}{4}$ pint double cream (lightly
   whipped)

*Ice cream churn freezer ; bombe
mould, or cake tin (about 1½ pints
capacity)*

1 *For Bombe Diane, the bombe
mould is lined with coffee cream ice*
2 *The centre of the mould is filled
with a banana and cream mixture*

Method

Slake the instant coffee with a
little of the single cream, then
add to the remainder of the
single cream and bring to
scalding point. Meanwhile break
the egg and egg yolks well with
a fork and add the caster sugar.
Pour on the hot coffee-flavoured
cream, then strain, cover the
basin and leave until cold. Whip
the double cream lightly and
add to the cold coffee cream
mixture.

Note : at this point the mixture
may be refrigerated overnight.

Have ready the freezer packed
with ice and salt (see page 52),
pour in the mixture and churn
until firm. Then remove the
dasher, pack down and refill, if
necessary, with extra ice and
salt, first pouring off any water.

Have the bombe mould (or
cake tin) well iced (put it into the
refrigerator 1 hour before you
want to use it). Slice the bananas, sprinkle with lemon juice
(or rum) and dust well with
icing sugar. Fold in the whipped
cream. When ready to pack,
line the sides of the mould (or
tin) with the cream ice. Fill the
centre at once with bananas
and cream. Cover with any remaining cream ice and, if using
a bombe mould, put on the lid
(cover tin with greaseproof paper
and foil). Bury bombe mould in
ice and salt (or put tin into ice-
making compartment of refrigerator if this is large enough, or
home-freezer). Leave 3-4 hours
or longer (2-3 hours for home-
freezer), then turn out by dipping
mould or tin into cold water.
Wipe round the mould and turn
bombe on to a chilled dish.

Serve Bombe Diane on a silver dish for maximum effect

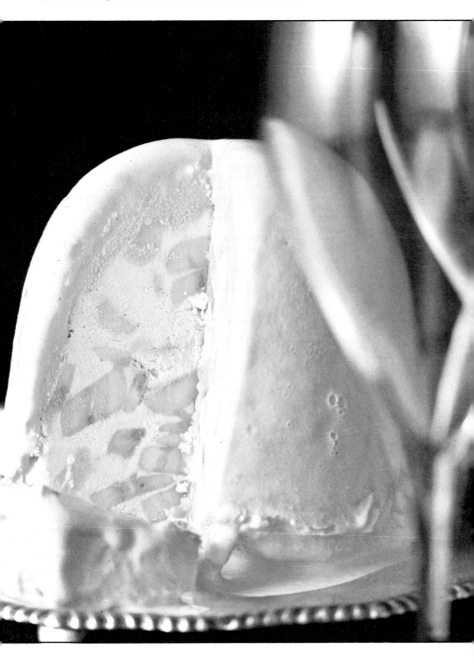

Bombe maison

1 jar of preserved ginger
½ pint double cream

For meringue
3 egg whites
6 oz caster sugar

For white coffee cream ice
½ pint single cream
2 oz coffee beans
1 whole egg
1 egg yolk
2 oz caster sugar
½ pint double cream

6-7 inch diameter cake tin with a loose bottom

This recipe is sometimes called meringue glacé maison when made in a cake tin; it can be made in a bombe mould but you will find that the meringue rounds fit a cake tin better.

Method
Line three baking sheets with non-stick silicone kitchen paper on which you have drawn three 5½-inch diameter circles. Set oven at 250°F or Mark ½.

To prepare the meringue: whisk egg whites until stiff and add 3 teaspoons of the measured sugar and continue beating for 1 minute. Fold in the remaining sugar with a tablespoon and then spread or pipe the mixture on to the three circles on the prepared baking sheets. Bake in pre-set oven for about 1 hour, or until meringues are dry, crisp and pale biscuit-coloured.

To prepare coffee cream ice: scald the single cream with the coffee beans and infuse until a delicate coffee flavour is obtained. Cream the egg and the extra yolk thoroughly with the sugar until light in colour, strain on the scalded cream and whisk well; strain again and leave to cool. Whip the double cream very slightly and add to the coffee-flavoured custard.

Meanwhile have churn ready packed with ice and salt. Pour in the custard mixture and churn until thick. Scrape down the container, remove the dasher and leave the mixture to ripen.

Slice the preserved ginger; whip the cream until thick and fold in the ginger. When the meringue is quite cold line the cake tin with a 1-inch layer of the coffee cream ice, put a round of meringue on the top and cover with a layer of cream and ginger. Continue in this way until the tin is full, filling any space at the sides with cream ice. Cover with foil and keep in the ice-making compartment of a refrigerator, or home-freezer (or a pail of ice, if using a bombe mould), until needed. Remove to refrigerator temperature for 1-2 hours before serving.

Cassata

1 pint vanilla cream ice (see page 58)
1 pint chocolate cream ice (see page 59)
¼ pint double cream (whipped)
4-5 tablespoons mixed chopped glacé fruit (soaked in 2 tablespoons rum)

Bombe mould (1¼-1½ pints capacity), or 7-8 inch diameter cake tin

Method
Have the well chilled mould or tin ready. Line it with the vanilla cream ice, then line again with the chocolate cream ice ; keep some vanilla cream ice aside. Fill the centre with the macerated glacé fruit mixed with the whipped cream, then top with the remaining cream ice. Put a piece of foil over top and freeze, preferably in a home-freezer for 6 hours, or in the ice-making compartment of a refrigerator if it is turned to its lowest temperature. Freeze for 6 hours or longer (preferably overnight) in refrigerator.

Dip the bombe or tin into cold water and turn out the cassata. Cut it into slices for serving.

Cassata, of Neapolitan origin, is made of layers of vanilla and chocolate cream ice with chopped glacé fruit mixed with whipped cream in centre

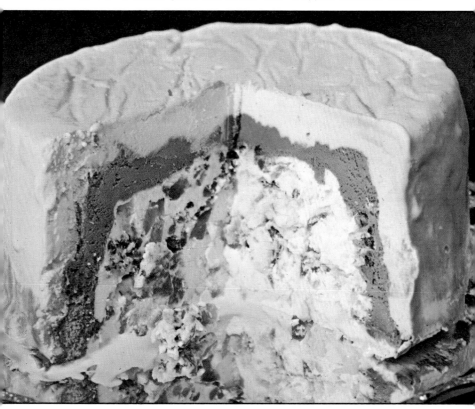

Strawberries Jeanne Granier

1¼ lb strawberries
icing sugar
2-3 tablespoons Grand
  Marnier, or curaçao
orange water ice (quantity as for
  recipe on page 55)

For curaçao mousse
3 egg yolks (well beaten)
3 oz granulated sugar
4 fl oz water
2-3 tablespoons curaçao, or
  Grand Marnier
7½ fl oz – ½ pint double cream
  (whipped)

Glass serving bowl

This quantity serves six. Should
you wish to serve it as a parfait, use 2 oz sugar only; put it
in a bombe mould (1½ pints
capacity) and deep-freeze for
4 hours.

Method

Hull strawberries, dust with
icing sugar and sprinkle with
the liqueur, then chill.

To prepare mousse: boil the
sugar and water until the thread
stage is reached (see method,
Coffee parfait, right), pour on to
the well beaten yolks. Whisk until
thick, then continue to whisk
over ice until really cold. Add the
liqueur, fold in the same quantity (volume) of whipped cream
as mousse. Keep in ice-making
compartment of the refrigerator
until ready to serve.

Have a well chilled glass
bowl ready for serving.

Watchpoint Do not leave the
glass bowl in the refrigerator for
too long because it will crack.
You may find it easier to pack
ice from the churn bucket
around the bowl.

Place the orange water ice in
the bottom, cover with the
strawberries and their juice, then
cover with the curaçao mousse.
Serve immediately.

Watchpoint It is important that
the same quantity (volume)
of whipped cream as mousse
is added, otherwise it will
not stand up well on the
strawberries.

Jeanne Granier was a
French actress, born in
Paris in 1852, who shone
in light operetta and comedy
roles.

Coffee parfait

4 egg yolks
2 tablespoons instant coffee
3 oz lump, or granulated, sugar
scant 4 fl oz water
$\frac{1}{2}$ pint single cream and $\frac{1}{2}$ pint double
cream, or 1 pint double cream

*Bombe mould (1$\frac{1}{2}$ pints capacity),
or 9-inch diameter cake tin (lined
with foil)*

Method
Work egg yolks with the instant coffee. Dissolve the sugar in the water over gentle heat, then boil it up well until it reaches the thread stage (ie. when a little cooled syrup will form a thread between your finger and thumb). Draw pan aside and wait until the bubbles have subsided, then pour sugar mixture on to the yolk mixture and whisk with a rotary whisk until it is a thick mousse. Leave it to cool.

Gradually add the single cream, or half the double cream if using double only. Whip the second $\frac{1}{2}$ pint double cream until it will just drop from the whisk, then fold it into the mixture.

Pour the mixture into the bombe mould or tin, cover the top with a piece of greaseproof paper, then secure the lid. Bury in a large bowl of ice and salt and leave for 3-4 hours, pouring off the water at intervals and replenishing with ice. Or stand bombe mould in a home-freezer, or the ice-making compartment of the refrigerator. Treat the cake tin in the same way, but do not bury in ice and salt, just freeze it in the ice-making compartment.

Chestnut parfait

1 can (16 oz) sweetened
chestnut purée
$\frac{1}{2}$ pint custard (made with 4 egg yolks,
1 oz granulated sugar, $\frac{1}{2}$ pint milk
and 1 vanilla pod — see method)
1 pint double cream
3-4 tablespoons maraschino
$\frac{1}{4}$ lb packet candied chocolate
orange sticks (cut in pieces)
double cream (whipped) — for
masking
marrons glacés debris (optional)

*7-8 inch diameter cake tin, or fluted
jelly mould (2$\frac{1}{2}$ pints capacity)*

Method
To make the custard : put vanilla pod in milk and leave, covered, to infuse over low heat for 7-10 minutes, until it reaches scalding point. Meanwhile, cream egg yolks with sugar in a bowl. Strain milk on to yolk mixture and blend. Return to pan over gentle heat and stir continually with a wooden spoon. When custard coats the spoon, strain back into bowl. Leave to cool. Whip the cream until just thickening, then add the maraschino. Blend the chestnut purée, custard and cream together, add about half the orange sticks.

Turn into the mould, cover with foil and freezer paper, and tie in a polythene bag and freeze in the ice compartment of refrigerator.

Serve masked with cream and decorated with marrons glacés debris (broken pieces) and the remaining candied orange sticks.

Mango ice

1 can (20 oz) mangoes
pared rind and juice of 1 lemon
4 tablespoons granulated sugar
$\frac{1}{4}$ pint water

Method
Drain the syrup from the mangoes into a measure and set aside. Then crush the mangoes well with a fork.

Note : if wished, reserve some of the mangoes for decoration.

Put the pared rind of the lemon into a pan with the sugar and water. Bring slowly to the boil and boil for 3-4 minutes (this should give $7\frac{1}{2}$ fl oz sugar syrup). Add the strained juice of the lemon, remove the rind and pour this liquid into the measure containing the mango syrup. Stir in the crushed mangoes. (There should now be about $1\frac{1}{2}$ pints in all.)

Chill this mixture thoroughly, then pour into ice trays and put in the freezing compartment of the refrigerator. Leave for 2-3 hours, stirring well occasionally. Serve in coupe glasses; if wished, top each with 1-2 pieces of reserved mango.

Grapefruit mousse

2 cans (6 fl oz each) frozen
   grapefruit juice
2 egg whites
4 rounded tablespoons caster sugar

Method
Take the grapefruit juice out of the ice-making compartment of the refrigerator, or the freezer, for about 1 hour before using. Open and turn out; by this time it should be a slush. Whip the egg whites stiffly, add the sugar and continue to whisk until firm, then gradually add the grapefruit juice, whisking all the time. Do this with an electric mixer if possible. Turn into coupe glasses for serving.

Jellies and charlottes

Cool and clear, or cool and milky — the essence of summer desserts. Whether you choose to serve a simple jelly, shivering lightly on its dish, or the more elaborate charlotte, cased in langues de chats biscuits or sponge fingers, both are hot weather winners.

For a cool evening party, when you can take advantage of the long summer days to eat out of doors, or as a dessert to a more formal meal, savour the contrasting textures of a home-made charlotte — crisp biscuits or sponge on the outside and a smooth, smooth cream or purée in the centre. Or a jelly, just barely set and dissolving on your tongue.

As host, or hostess, remember that a jelly should never be set too firm or it will be unpalatable. And it is also better if not served straight from the refrigerator; the cold detracts from the flavour and will leave your guests with their teeth on edge.

Any number of delicious jellies can be made from the rich variety of summer fruits. The basic jelly used for them all is the lemon one given overleaf — it is light and tasty and will complement any fruit you put with it.

Lemon jelly

1¾ oz gelatine
1½ pints water
pared rind of 3 lemons
7½ fl oz lemon juice
2 sticks cinnamon
7 oz lump sugar
whites and shells (wiped and
    lightly crushed) of 2 eggs
2½ fl oz sherry, or water

This basic recipe makes 2 pints of lemon jelly.

Method
Soak gelatine in $\frac{1}{4}$ pint of the water. Scald a large enamel pan, or an aluminium one with a ground base (use 6 pints capacity pan to allow for boiling). Pour in remaining $1\frac{1}{4}$ pints of water, add the lemon rind and juice, cinnamon and sugar; warm over gentle heat until sugar is dissolved.

Whip egg whites to a froth, add to the pan with the shells, gelatine and sherry, or water.

Whisk until liquid reaches boiling point, with a backwards (the reverse of the usual whisking movement) and downwards movement. Stop whisking at once and allow liquid to rise well in the pan. At once turn off heat or draw pan aside and leave liquid to settle for about 5 minutes. Bring liquid to the boil two more times, without whisking and drawing pan aside between each boiling to allow it to settle.

By this time a 'filter', or thick white crust, will have formed on top of the liquid. It will be cracked, so that the liquid below is visible. If the liquid is clear, carry on to the next stage; if it is muddy-looking, bring it to the boil once more.

Have ready a scalded jelly bag with a bowl underneath and turn the contents of the pan into it. Once the jelly begins to run through, take up the bowl (placing another underneath) and pour jelly back into the bag. After a few times the jelly running through should be crystal clear. Then allow it to run through completely before moving bag or bowl. A screw-top jar or jug of hot water placed in the bag helps to keep the jelly liquid.

Watchpoint Lump sugar is best for jelly-making; it will give a more brilliant jelly as it is less adulterated than the powdered sugar.

Fruit jelly madeleine

about 1¼ pints lemon jelly (see page 72)
fresh fruit (black grapes, cherries, or strawberries)

For vanilla cream
2 egg yolks
1 dessertspoon caster sugar
¼ pint milk
3-4 tablespoons water
¼ oz gelatine
2-3 drops of vanilla essence
3¾ fl oz double cream (lightly whipped)

Charlotte tin, or glass bowl (about 1¾-2 pints capacity)

Method

Have ready the tin or bowl. Pour in cold jelly to cover base by ¼-½ inch. Arrange the fruit on this and set with a little jelly and put aside.

To prepare the vanilla cream: cream the yolks with the sugar, scald the milk, pour on to the eggs, return to pan, thicken over heat without boiling. Add the water to the gelatine and, when soft, dissolve over a gentle heat. Add to the custard with a few drops of vanilla.

When custard is cool and on the point of setting, fold in the whipped cream. Pour mixture carefully on to the jellied fruit and leave to set. Add any left-over fruit to remaining jelly and spoon over the top to fill the tin or bowl completely.

Leave madeleine for 1-2 hours, then turn out and surround with chopped jelly.

Cherry and raspberry jelly

½ lb cherries
1 lb raspberries
½ lb redcurrants, or blackcurrants
1 pint water
2 oz fine sago
4-6 oz granulated sugar (to taste)
clotted cream (for serving)

Ring mould (1½ pints capacity)

Method

Stone the cherries (see page 32) and crack kernels; string currants. Put the fruit and kernels into a pan with the water. Cover and simmer gently until currants split and give out their juice; then rub mixture through a nylon strainer. Return to pan, add sago and sugar.

Boil mixture carefully until sago is cooked (about 3-5 minutes), taking care that it doesn't stick to the bottom of the pan. Pour into wet mould, leave to cool. Turn out and serve cold with clotted cream.

Fresh fruit jelly

2 clementines
1 ripe dessert pear
6 oz black, or white, grapes
$\frac{1}{2}$ lb lump sugar
1 pint water
finely pared rind and juice of
  1 lemon
$1\frac{1}{2}$ oz gelatine (soaked in $4\frac{1}{2}$ fl oz
  water)
1 can ($6\frac{1}{4}$ fl oz) concentrated frozen
  orange juice made up with
  14 fl oz water

Method

Put the sugar and water in a pan with the lemon rind and juice. Dissolve over gentle heat, then simmer for 5 minutes. Strain this syrup through muslin, wringing it out very well to remove all the syrup and essence from the lemon rind. Add the soaked gelatine to the hot syrup and stir until completely dissolved.

Watchpoint It is important to have the gelatine soaking in the cold water before the sugar syrup is prepared. It should be added to the hot syrup as soon as this has been strained.

Add the diluted orange juice to the sugar syrup and gelatine mixture and allow to cool.

Peel and slice the clementines; peel, core and slice the ripe pears; skin and pip the grapes. Arrange the fruit in a glass bowl and pour on cool jelly. Cover and allow to set.

Serve a bowl of whipped cream with the jelly.

Coffee jelly

1 pint strong black coffee (made with ground coffee beans, or freeze-dried instant coffee)
1 oz gelatine
$2\frac{1}{2}$ fl oz water
2 oz granulated sugar
thinly pared rind of $\frac{1}{2}$ orange

For decoration
$2\frac{1}{2}$ fl oz double, or whipping, cream (whipped, sweetened and flavoured with vanilla essence), or pastry cream (see page 12)
2 oz flaked browned almonds

Method

Melt the gelatine in the water. Add the sugar and orange rind to the freshly made coffee and stir gently until the sugar is dissolved, then cover and leave to infuse for 10 minutes. Strain coffee through a double thickness of muslin, add the gelatine mixture and pour into a glass bowl. Leave to set.

Cover with the flavoured cream (or pastry cream); scatter over the browned almonds.

Almond jelly with lychees

2 oz almonds (blanched, dried and put through a fine nut mill)
1 pint warm water
¼ pint evaporated milk
3 tablespoons caster sugar
1 oz gelatine (soaked in 4 tablespoons water)
a few drops of almond essence
1 can of lychees (in their syrup)

Method
Infuse the milled almonds in the warm water for 30 minutes, then strain through fine muslin. Mix this almond milk with the evaporated milk and the sugar in a pan and heat gently to dissolve the sugar ; cool a little.

Melt the soaked gelatine gently and then stir into the warm milk mixture until dissolved. Cool, add almond essence to taste. Pour into a shallow dish and put in the refrigerator to set until firm. Cut the jelly into diamonds about 1 inch wide and serve in a bowl with the lychees and their syrup.

Pineapple charlotte

1 pint milk
4 egg yolks
1 teaspoon arrowroot
2 rounded tablespoons caster sugar
1 medium-size can pineapple rings
½ pint double cream
scant ¾ oz powdered gelatine
2 egg whites
1 packet langues de chats biscuits

7-inch diameter spring-form cake tin (a catch unclips to open sides)

Method
Scald milk in a pan. Cream egg yolks in a bowl with arrowroot and sugar, pour on milk and return to pan. Stir over heat to thicken, but do not boil. Strain custard and cool.

Drain pineapple (keep juice) ; chop up 2 rings (to give 3-4 tablespoons of chopped pineapple) and keep rest for decoration. Lightly whip cream.

Soak gelatine in 4 tablespoons pineapple juice, dissolve over heat, then add to custard with three-quarters of cream. Whisk egg whites until stiff.

As custard begins to thicken, fold in egg whites with chopped pineapple, using a metal spoon. Turn at once into cake tin. When set, turn out and spread sides of charlotte with remaining cream ; arrange biscuits, upright, on cream, overlapping slightly. Decorate top with rest of pineapple and additional cream.

Charlotte russe

1 pint lemon jelly (see page 72)
few glacé cherries
few diamonds of angelica
12 sponge fingers (ready made)

For Bavarian cream
½ pint milk
1 vanilla pod, or 2-3 drops of
   vanilla essence
3 egg yolks
1 rounded tablespoon caster sugar
¾ oz gelatine
   (soaked in 3 tablespoons water)
1½ pint double cream

Charlotte tin (1½ pints capacity)

This is the name given to a cold sweet that is set in a plain round mould (similar to a deep cake tin) with gently sloping sides widening out at the top. Bavarian cream (bavarois) is a rich egg custard stiffened or set with gelatine, and whipped cream added.

Charlotte russe was created by the famous early 19th century chef Carème while he was in Paris, where it first graced the tables of Foreign Ministers and Ministers of Security.

Method

Prepare the jelly and when cool, but still liquid, pour a little into the bottom of the charlotte tin to the depth of ¼ inch. Leave to set. Arrange a pattern of cherries and angelica on this layer and set carefully with a little more jelly.

Keep remaining jelly for decoration. Trim the sides of the sponge fingers and fit closely round the sides of the tin (see right).

To prepare the Bavarian cream: scald the milk with the vanilla pod and leave to infuse (to absorb the flavour), but if using vanilla essence do not add yet. Cream the egg yolks and sugar until light in texture. Pour the milk, removing the vanilla pod, on to egg mixture; return to the pan and stir over heat until the resulting custard coats the back of a spoon.

Watchpoint Do not boil or the mixture will curdle. If this does happen, quickly tip the mixture into a large, cold mixing bowl and whisk vigorously for 1-2 minutes.

Strain custard mixture into a bowl, add the soaked gelatine, stir until dissolved and then allow to cool. If using vanilla essence, add at this point.

Then whip the cream very lightly with a wire whisk or fork. Return mixture to a saucepan and stand this in another bowl of cold water in which there are a few ice cubes. Stir gently until it starts to thicken evenly. Quickly fold whipped cream into the mixture. Pour at once into the prepared charlotte tin, cover with foil, or a plate, and leave to set in the refrigerator. (All dairy produce will pick up other flavours in a refrigerator so never leave uncovered.)

For serving, dip the bottom of the mould quickly in and out of hot water, turn carefully on to a plate (traditionally of silver but any decorative one will do). Chop any remaining jelly and spoon it around the charlotte russe.

Before the Bavarian cream filling is added, set a little of the jelly in the bottom of the charlotte tin. Then arrange on this a pattern of cherries and angelica, and set in place with more jelly. Trim the sponge fingers to fit and arrange them round the tin

Banana chartreuse

1½ pints lemon jelly
about 12 pistachio nuts
(blanched — see page 154) —
optional
3 bananas

Ring mould (1¼-1½ pints capacity)

Method
Have ready the jelly, which should be cool but not set. Stand the mould in a roasting tin, pour round a little cold water and add a few ice cubes.

Turn the jelly into a bowl, stand this in water with ice cubes and stir gently with a metal spoon until the jelly is cold to the touch but not set. Spoon in enough jelly to cover the bottom of the mould to a depth of $\frac{1}{4}$ - $\frac{1}{2}$ inch. Leave to set.

Blanch and finely chop the pistachio nuts. Slice bananas. Place nuts on a layer of jelly, pour a little more over, and when set arrange a single layer of bananas on the top, set this with a little more jelly and repeat this process until mould is full, the last layer being of jelly. Leave for at least 1½-2 hours to set. Then turn out chartreuse and fill the centre with chopped jelly.

Serve a bowl of whipped cream separately.

Apricot charlotte

1 lb apricots (stoned)
sugar syrup (made with ¾ cup water
    and 2 rounded tablespoons
    granulated sugar)
3 tablespoons caster sugar
¼–½ oz gelatine
6 tablespoons water
½ pint double cream (whipped)

For serving
¼ pint double cream (whipped)
1 packet langues de chats biscuits

*7-inch diameter cake tin (lightly
oiled)*

Method
Make the sugar syrup and poach
apricots in it until tender (page
15), then strain ; reserve syrup.

Reserve 6 apricot halves for
decoration and rub the rest
through a strainer to a purée.
Measure this purée, make up to
¾ pint with the poaching syrup
and stir in the caster sugar.
Soak gelatine in the water then
dissolve it over gentle heat.
Add to apricot purée. Whip
cream lightly until it is just
beginning to hold shape.

Pour the apricot mixture into
a thin saucepan, stand this in
a bowl of cold water with a
few ice cubes added, and stir
until the mixture begins to
thicken. Fold in the cream and
pour into the prepared tin.
Cover and leave in a cool place
until set (about 2 hours).

To serve, turn out the charlotte, spread the biscuits with
whipped cream and overlap
them round the sides of the
charlotte. This will make the
biscuits fit better and stops
cream from oozing out between
them. Decorate top with rosettes
of cream and the reserved
apricot halves.

Strawberry charlotte

7 ½ fl oz strawberry purée (made by rubbing strawberries through a nylon strainer)
3 eggs
2 yolks
6 oz caster sugar
½ pint double cream
½ oz gelatine
juice of ½ lemon (made up to 2½ fl oz with water)

To finish
¼ pint double cream
langues de chats biscuits
angelica (cut into diamonds)

7½-8 inch diameter shallow cake tin (preferably spring - form or loose bottom)

Method
Put the eggs, yolks and sugar in a bowl and whisk over gentle heat (or without heat, using an electric mixer at high speed) until thick and mousse-like. Half whip the cream and dissolve the gelatine in the lemon juice and water over gentle heat. Add the strawberry purée, gelatine and cream to the mousse and stir over ice until it thickens creamily.

Pour into the cake tin, lined with foil, cover and leave to set.

To serve, whip the cream and sweeten very lightly. Spread the biscuits with cream and press overlapping around the charlotte, decorate with rosettes of cream and diamonds of angelica.

Charlotte mexicaine

2 oz coffee beans
1 pint milk
6 oz block chocolate
5 egg yolks
2 oz granulated sugar
½ oz gelatine (dissolved in 2½ fl oz water)
7½ fl oz double cream
1 egg white

For decoration
langues de chats biscuits
¼-½ pint double cream
squares, or rounds, of chocolate (optional) — see pages 26, 126

7-8 inch diameter cake tin (oiled)

Method
Infuse coffee beans in the milk for 10-12 minutes over gentle heat without boiling. Cut up chocolate, put into a pan and strain on a little of the coffee-flavoured milk. Dissolve chocolate over gentle heat, strain on rest of milk and blend well.

Work the egg yolks and sugar well together, pour on the milk and chocolate mixture, stir to blend and return to the pan. Stir until the custard will coat the back of the spoon but do not allow it to boil; strain and leave it to cool.

Add gelatine liquid to custard, turn it into a thin pan; set this in a bowl of cold water or on ice. When it is on the point of setting, partially whip the cream, whisk egg white, add it to cream, then fold both into the chocolate. Turn this into the prepared tin and leave to set.

Turn out charlotte. Lightly whip remaining cream and spread a little over sides of charlotte; press on biscuits, slightly overlapping. Decorate top with cream and chocolate.

Soufflés and mousses

Summer is a time to relax, to eat out of doors and, as far as possible, to keep away from the hot stove. So when you have a dinner party coming up, make your treat a cool one.

Cold soufflés and mousses are ideal. Incidentally, they are also a convenient way of utilising fruit that is past its best, or has never had a best. So long as you cut away any part that is actually damaged, it will not matter that the fruit is imperfect, since to purée it you will rub it through a fine nylon sieve anyway. (You can of course use a blender / liquidiser to purée fruits, but you will still need to sieve out any seeds or skin afterwards to make it truly smooth.)

A cold mousse is made with whole eggs plus extra egg yolks, beaten together with sugar until thick, purée flavouring added, and the whole enriched with cream and lightly set with gelatine. The end product is rich and delicious.

For a cold sweet soufflé, the eggs are always separated, the yolks are beaten with the sugar and flavourings (which may be purée or juice) until thick, or made into a custard with milk if cream is to be added. You then whisk the egg whites stiffly, fold them gently into the mixture and set it lightly with melted gelatine.

A cold soufflé is particularly exciting to present for a more formal dinner party. Even though it is not cooked, it is always dressed up to look like a hot soufflé that has risen above the edge of its dish in the baking! To produce this effect the dish is prepared with a band of double greaseproof paper tied round the outside, standing up an inch or so above the dish to support the gelatine mixture until it has set. The paper support is important because the correct amount of gelatine will not support more than about an inch of soufflé mixture above the edge of the dish — if you find your mixture will stand higher than that, you are using too much gelatine and the soufflé is too firmly set. To remove the paper case, hold a palette knife under the hot tap and, while it is still warm, run it between the two layers of greaseproof paper. This will just melt the jelly that clings to the paper and allow you to peel it off without damage.

For a perfect soufflé the egg whites must be whisked by hand with a light wire whisk. A rotary beater makes them too solid, so that by the time they are mixed into the soufflé they have lost a lot of bulk. (For mousses, a rotary, or electric, beater is more satisfactory as the whole eggs are beaten.)

If you are adding cream to either soufflés or mousses, whip that lightly too ; lift a little on the whisk, or fork, and it should leave a trail across the remaining cream. This helps to give the finished sweet its spongy texture.

One final point to remember: gelatine sweets are not good if they have been made more than a day. Soufflés, particularly, lose their lightness and life, as the 'set' becomes stiffer and stiffer. So if you are preparing for a dinner party, don't make the dessert before the morning of the same day.

Soufflé Monte Cristo

3 eggs (separated)
2½ oz granulated sugar
½ vanilla pod (split)
¾ pint milk
2-3 drops of vanilla essence
    (optional)
½ oz gelatine
2¼ fl oz water
7½ fl oz double cream (lightly
    whipped)
chocolate caraque (made from
    2 oz plain block chocolate — see
    page 153)
5 almond macaroons
little brandy, or rum, or liqueur
    (such as Cointreau, or Grand
    Marnier)
¼ pint double cream (more if liked)
    — for decoration

*6-inch diameter top (No. 2 size)
soufflé dish ; ½ lb jam jar*

*The thickened soufflé mixture and
chocolate caraque are layered into
the prepared soufflé dish, with the
jam jar in the centre to form cavity*

Method

Prepare the soufflé dish ; lightly oil the jam jar and put it in the centre of the soufflé dish. Put the egg yolks into a basin and beat with the sugar until light and fluffy, while infusing vanilla pod in the milk in a pan. When at scalding point, remove pod and pour the milk on to the yolk mixture. Return to the pan and stir over gentle heat until the custard thickens creamily and will coat the back of the spoon. Strain and cool. If necessary, add 2-3 drops of vanilla essence to strengthen the flavour.

Soak and dissolve the gelatine in the water and add to the custard. Turn the mixture into a thin pan and stand this on ice, or in iced water, and stir with a metal spoon until the mixture is thickening. Then remove from the ice and fold in the lightly whipped cream and, finally, the stiffly whisked egg whites. Pour the soufflé mixture quickly into the dish, layering it with chocolate caraque, keeping some in reserve for decoration. Leave in a cool place, or in the refrigerator, to set.

Watchpoint A lump or two of ice put into the jam jar will help the soufflé to set more quickly if you are pressed for time.

Meanwhile break up the macaroons and sprinkle them well with the chosen liqueur. When ready to serve, gently twist the jam jar and lift it out carefully. Immediately fill the cavity with the macaroons. Peel away paper, pipe the extra whipped cream round the edge and decorate with chocolate caraque.

Cold chocolate soufflé

4 oz plain block chocolate
(roughly chopped)
good ½ pint milk
3 eggs
2 oz caster sugar
5 tablespoons water, or black
coffee
½ oz gelatine
¼ pint double cream

To decorate
¼ pint double cream
1 oz plain block chocolate (grated)

*6-inch diameter top (No. 2 size)
soufflé dish*

*To prepare the soufflé case, take a
piece of double thickness greaseproof paper, turn up bottom edge,
and tie paper securely round case*

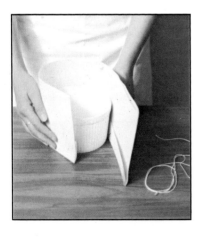

Method
Prepare soufflé dish.

Put ¼ pint of milk into a large pan with the 4 oz chopped chocolate and dissolve over very gentle heat.

Watchpoint Do not let the milk reach more than blood heat (just warm) until the chocolate has melted or the texture will not be smooth.

Add remaining milk to the pan and bring to scalding (just under boiling) point.

Separate the egg whites from yolks. Work yolks with sugar until thick and light. Tip the chocolate-flavoured milk on to mixture. Return this chocolate custard mixture to saucepan and stir over gentle heat until mixture thickens and coats the back of a wooden spoon. Do not boil. Strain into a large bowl or metal pan and allow to cool. (The metal will allow mixture to cool more quickly when pan is put on ice to set gelatine.)

Put water or coffee in a sauce-pan, add gelatine to soak, then dissolve over gentle heat and stir it quickly into the cold custard.

Lightly whip the first ¼ pint of cream. Whisk the egg whites until stiff. Stand bowl or pan of custard on ice, stir until just beginning to set (it is important to stir from time to time to thicken mixture evenly). Quickly fold in the cream and egg whites, using a metal spoon.

Watchpoint You must fold in the cream and egg whites as soon as mixture begins to set or they will not blend in completely.

Pour into soufflé dish immediately, leave in a cool place to finish setting.

To decorate : whip remaining

If you stand the bowl of chocolate custard on a bed of ice, this will help it to set. Egg whites and cream should then be folded in very quickly

$\frac{1}{4}$ pint of cream until stiff and spoon on top of soufflé ; sprinkle with grated chocolate.

Before serving, remove paper band.

Cold raspberry soufflé

1 can (14$\frac{1}{2}$ oz) raspberries
1 oz granulated sugar
scant $\frac{1}{2}$ oz gelatine (soaked in a little of the juice from the raspberries)
4 egg whites
$\frac{1}{4}$ pint double cream
double cream (for decoration)
crystallised violets and rose petals

Method
Heat the contents of the can of raspberries with the sugar to boiling point, add soaked gelatine and stir until dissolved. Leave until cool and beginning to set, then beat the egg whites stiffly and whip the cream. Gradually mix the raspberry mixture with the cream, then fold in the egg whites lightly but thoroughly.

Pour mixture into a small soufflé dish, or a glass bowl, and leave to set. Decorate with cream and crystallised violets and rose petals.

Soufflé chinois

¾ pint milk
3 egg yolks
2 oz caster sugar
2 tablespoons syrup (from the
  preserved ginger)
½ oz gelatine (soaked in 4 tablespoons cold water)
¼ pint double cream
3 egg whites
2 tablespoons preserved ginger
  (sliced)

For decoration
few extra preserved ginger slices
pistachio nuts (finely chopped), or
almonds (browned) — optional

*6-inch diameter top (No. 2 size)
soufflé dish*

*The custard turned into a large, thin
pan resting on a bed of ice, which
helps to cool custard more quickly.
Half the cream, ginger and whisked
egg whites are folded in. The mixture is stirred until it begins to
thicken, when it should be turned
immediately into the soufflé dish*

Method
Prepare soufflé dish by tying a
double-thickness band of greaseproof paper round the outside
to stand 3 inches above top of
dish. Grease inside lightly.

Scald the milk in a pan. Beat
the egg yolks and sugar together
until thick and light in colour,
add the ginger syrup and pour
on the hot milk. Return to the
pan and stir over a gentle heat
until the mixture thickens. Strain
it into a bowl, add the soaked
gelatine and stir until it is
dissolved. Cover the bowl of
custard to prevent a skin forming
and allow to cool.

Whip the cream lightly until it
begins to thicken and whisk the
egg whites until stiff but not dry.
Turn the custard into a large thin
pan, stand this in a bowl of cold
water containing 3-4 ice cubes
and stir until the mixture begins
to thicken (a metal saucepan
cools it more quickly than a
china bowl).

Then take a metal spoon and
quickly fold in half the cream,
the sliced ginger and the
whisked egg whites. Stir very
carefully, holding the pan in the
ice-cold water, and as the mixture
begins to thicken, turn it
into the prepared soufflé dish
and put in a cool place to set.

When set, peel away the paper
around soufflé dish.

Whisk the remaining cream
and use to coat and decorate
the top of the soufflé. Sprinkle
with nuts, if wanted, and
arrange the extra ginger slices
around the top.

Soufflé chinois — half of the cream is used to decorate top, together with slices of preserved ginger. You may like to sprinkle with chopped nuts

Apricot soufflé

4 eggs (separated)
2 oz caster sugar
½ pint apricot purée (made from canned, or cooked fresh, or dried, apricots)
½ oz gelatine
5 tablespoons water if using fresh, or dried, apricots (or juice of ½ lemon and water to make 5 tablespoons if using canned apricots)
¼ pint double cream

For decoration
2½ fl oz double cream
pistachio nuts (chopped)

6-inch diameter top (No. 2 size) soufflé dish

Method
To purée apricots, rub through a nylon strainer, or work in a blender. Prepare soufflé dish.

Put egg yolks, sugar and purée in a basin over a pan of hot water and whisk until mixture has thickened a little. Remove basin from heat and continue whisking until bowl is cool and whisk leaves a trail.

Soak the gelatine in the water (or lemon juice and water) and dissolve over gentle heat. Whip cream until it just begins to thicken, then fold into soufflé mixture; add gelatine liquid. Whisk egg whites until stiff but not dry. Stand basin in a bowl of iced water and cut and fold in egg whites with a metal spoon. Stir mixture until it begins to thicken, then pour at once into prepared soufflé dish. Put in a cool place to set.

To serve: whip cream and sweeten slightly. Remove paper from soufflé and decorate with cream and nuts.

Gooseberry soufflé

½ pint gooseberry purée (made with 1 lb green gooseberries, ¼ pint water, 4 rounded tablespoons granulated sugar, 4-5 heads of elderflowers)
4 eggs (separated)
2 oz caster sugar
¼ pint double cream
½ oz gelatine
5 tablespoons water
2-3 drops of green colouring (optional)

For decoration
7 fl oz double cream (whipped)
browned almonds (finely chopped), or crushed ratafia crumbs

6-inch diameter top (No. 2 size) soufflé dish

Method
To purée gooseberries, cook (see method, Gooseberry fool, page 42) and rub through a nylon strainer, or work in a blender. Prepare soufflé dish.

Beat egg yolks, sugar and purée in a bowl. Whisk mixture over heat until thick, then remove from heat and continue whisking until bowl is cool.

Half whip the ¼ pint cream, stir into gooseberry mixture. Soak gelatine in water, then dissolve over gentle heat; add to soufflé with colouring. When mixture begins to thicken, whisk egg whites to a firm snow, fold in carefully with a metal spoon and turn soufflé into dish; leave it to set.

Decorate with whipped cream and the nuts or ratafia crumbs.

Crème Brûlée.

6 helpings.

½ pint peel milk.
½ pint cream,
5 eggs.
2 oz. Sugar.

Vanilla Essence or Brandy.
Icing Sugar.
Chopped, Blanched Almonds (opt)

1. Heat milk & cream until almost boiling.
2. Beat eggs & sugar together to blend well.
3. Pour on the hot milk & cream, stirring well,
4. Add vanilla or brandy to taste,
5. Strain into a 1½ pint fire proof china soufflé dish.

Magic Fondant.

8 oz Icing Sugar.
2 tablespoons condensed milk.

Sift icing sugar, mix with condensed milk
until smooth & creamy. You can flavour it with
peppermint or fruit flavouring. Shape the mixture
into sweets.

Coconut Ice

6 oz Coconut.   4 Tablespoons condensed milk.
12 oz Icing Sugar.

Mix together milk & icing sugar. Stir in the
coconut. Shape into sweets.

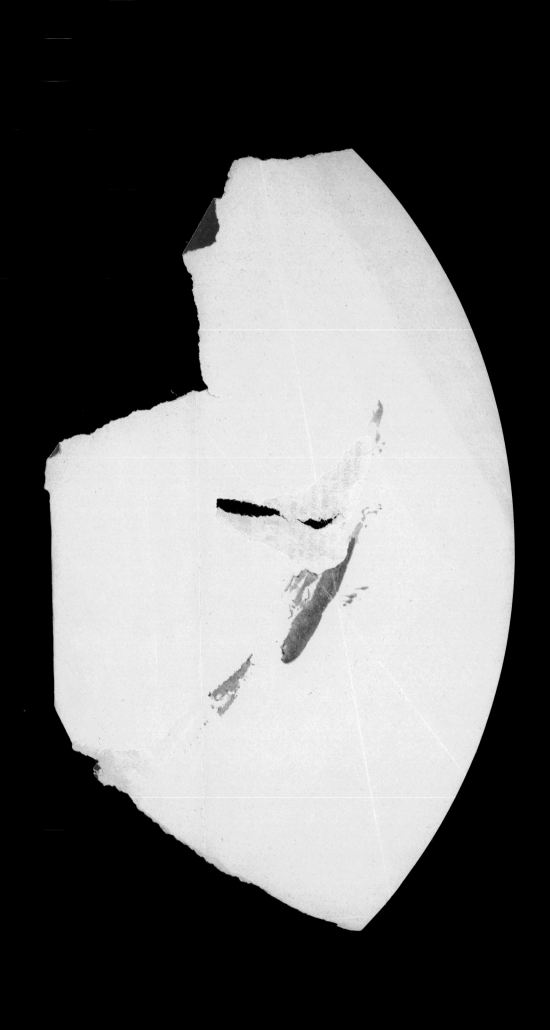

FOUR EGG PAVLOVA

Pavlova pan. Pan may be prepared several ways—lined with foil—Greased and dusted with 1 teaspoon cornflour—or lined with greaseproof paper. Pavlova pan with vanilla. Beat 1½ cups fine sugar, beating. Beat egg whites until stiff peaks are formed. Pile on prepared pan—or lined ways—Greased and prepared. Fold in half teaspoon cornflour, vinegar. Gradually add 1 teaspoon vanilla. Beat egg whites until soft peaks and lightly browned) for 1½ hours or until firm. Bake 250° on draughts. Spread Cool away from. Pavlova pan and vanilla until shape remaining stiff peaks are formed. Pile on prepared pan. Bake 250° on draughts. Cool away from firm. Cream and cover with whipped cream and cover with fruit. 275° (very slow oven) shape remaining stiff peaks. 1 teaspoon icing sugar, cornflour, Pavlova. Pan will take a 6 or 8 egg Pavlova—or lined ways—Greased mixed with 1 teaspoon cornflour.

6. ... very gentry ... in the
oven. Use a water bath if oven is hotter than 130°C,
265°F; Gas ½.

7. When set allow to cool a check the surface to a depth
of ⅛ ins with icing sugar.

8. Sprinkle chopped almonds over lightly, if liked,

9. Grill until sugar has been changed to caramel.

10. Serve cold with whipped cream,

Note. This recipe may be varied by substituting 1 pint cream for
½ pint of skim milk or ½ pt of cream, a using 6 egg yolks instead
of 5 whole eggs. Proceed as above.

Cold lemon soufflé

3 large, or 4 medium-size eggs
  (separated)
8 oz caster sugar
rind and juice of 2½ lemons
½ oz gelatine (soaked in 5 tablespoons cold water)
½ pint double cream
pistachio nuts, or browned
  almonds (finely chopped)
extra double cream (whipped) —
  for decoration

*6-inch diameter top (No. 2 size)
soufflé dish*

Method

Prepare soufflé dish.

Put the egg yolks, sugar, finely grated lemon rind and juice in a basin over a pan of hot water and whisk until the sugar has dissolved and the mixture has thickened a little. Remove the basin from the pan and continue whisking until the basin is cool.

Whip the egg yolks, sugar, lemon rind and juice until you see that the mixture begins to thicken

Dissolve the gelatine in a pan over gentle heat. Whip the cream until it just begins to thicken and the whisk leaves a trail, then fold it into the soufflé mixture. Add the dissolved gelatine. Whisk the egg whites until stiff but not dry.

Stand the soufflé mixture in a bowl of cold water containing a few ice cubes. Cut and fold in the egg whites very carefully with a metal spoon. Stir the mixture until it begins to thicken, then pour at once into the prepared soufflé dish. Put in a cool place to set.

For serving, remove the paper and decorate the top with whipped cream and nuts.

Tangerine mousse

3 eggs
2 egg yolks
3 oz caster sugar
scant $\frac{3}{4}$ oz gelatine
2 tablespoons cold water
juice of 1 lemon (strained)
$\frac{1}{4}$ pint double cream
6 fl oz tangerine juice
grated rind of 3 tangerines

For decoration
little extra double cream
chocolate squares (see page 26),
    or chopped walnuts

Method
Have ready a pan half full of boiling water with a pudding basin on top, making sure that the basin will sit on the pan without touching the water.

Whisk the whole eggs and yolks together in the basin, whisk in caster sugar in a steady stream. Remove pan from heat and whisk until the mixture is thick. When lifted on the whisk, the mixture should fall in a ribbon and hold its shape for 1-2 seconds. Remove basin from heat and whisk until cold. If using electric beater, use at high speed with no heat.

Soak the gelatine in the water in a pan, then add the strained lemon juice; dissolve gelatine over heat. Lightly whip the cream and add to the egg mixture with the tangerine juice, rind and gelatine. Stand basin in a bowl filled with ice and stir continuously until mixture thickens (this stirring should prevent uneven thickening) then pour quickly into a soufflé dish or glass bowl and leave to set.

Decorate with a little extra whipped cream and chocolate squares or chopped walnuts.

Decorate tangerine mousse with chocolate squares and whipped cream, or with a lattice pattern of cream and with chopped walnuts

Note : If using an electric beater at high speed to mix mousses it is not necessarry to do it over a pan of hot water.

Orange mousse

3 eggs
2 egg yolks
4 oz caster sugar
$\frac{1}{2}$ oz gelatine
juice of $\frac{1}{2}$ lemon (made up to 5
    tablespoons with water)
1 can orange juice (frozen)
$\frac{1}{4}$ pint double cream (lightly whipped)

The success of this mousse depends on the quick blending of these ingredients, so before you start mixing, collect everything together. See that the gelatine is soaking in the lemon juice and water in a small pan, open the can of orange juice but keep it in the refrigerator. Choose your prettiest glass bowl for serving.

Method
Whisk the whole eggs, egg yolks and sugar together until very thick; the mousse is ready when a little lifted on the whisk holds its shape as it falls in a spiral.

Dissolve the gelatine in the lemon juice and water over gentle heat; let it get quite hot but not to boiling point. Mix this into the egg mousse, then quickly add the orange juice and cream; blend together, using a large metal spoon.

If the orange juice is ice-cold, the mixture will begin to set almost immediately. As this happens, turn mousse into the glass bowl, cover with foil and put in refrigerator to set (about 30 minutes).

This mousse is very rich, so serve it plain.

Apricot mousse Basque

$\frac{1}{2}$ lb dried apricots (soaked
    overnight)
pared rind and juice of $\frac{1}{2}$ lemon
granulated sugar (to taste)
3-4 egg whites
thin squares of chocolate (see page
    26), or nougat

Method
Stew the apricots in the soaking liquid, with the lemon rind and juice, until very tender (for about 30 minutes), then add sugar to taste and cook for a further 5-10 minutes. Rub apricots through a sieve, or purée them in a blender; leave to cool.

Whip the egg whites until stiff, add to the apricot purée, a little at a time, and continue whisking until stiff. Pile in a serving dish and surround with chocolate (or nougat).

Bramble mousse

1 lb blackberries
1 oz caster sugar
3 eggs
3 oz caster sugar
$\frac{1}{2}$ oz gelatine
juice of $\frac{1}{2}$ lemon
2 tablespoons water
$\frac{1}{4}$ pint double cream

To decorate
3-4 fl oz double cream
caster sugar (to sweeten)

Method
Pick over the blackberries, put them in a saucepan with 1 oz caster sugar and stew gently until soft and pulpy. Rub them through a nylon strainer and leave to cool.

Whisk the eggs and remaining sugar together in a basin over a pan of hot water. Continue beating until basin is cold.

Watchpoint The mixture must be so thick that when a little is lifted on the whisk it should remain in a thick ribbon or rope on itself for 1 minute.

Soak the gelatine in the lemon juice and water, then dissolve it over gentle heat.

Lightly whip the cream until it is exactly the same consistency as the egg and sugar mixture. To the egg mixture add 6 fl oz of the blackberry purée, the gelatine and cream and fold together quickly but lightly. Stir the mixture over ice until it begins to thicken, then pour it quickly into a glass bowl; cover and leave for 1-2 hours in a cool place to set. Just before serving, spoon the remaining purée over the top of the mousse. Whip and sweeten the extra cream and pipe it in a lattice over the top.

Maple mousse

12 oz maple syrup
scant $\frac{1}{2}$ oz gelatine (soaked in 3 tablespoons cold water)
6 egg yolks
1$\frac{3}{4}$ pints double cream
1-2 oz flaked, or chopped, or toasted, almonds (for decoration)
1 tablespoon rum

This dish will serve 8.

Method
Heat the maple syrup in a double boiler and, when hot, add the soaked gelatine and stir until dissolved. Beat the egg yolks until very light, add a little of the hot syrup to them and then mix all the egg yolk into the syrup mixture.

When the syrup mixture is cool, whip the cream and fold in 1$\frac{1}{2}$ pints; pour into a glass bowl and put in the refrigerator to set — allow 2 hours for this. Cover the top with the almonds and serve with the remaining whipped cream flavoured with the rum.

Chocolate mousse basque

6 oz plain block chocolate
2-3 tablespoons water, or black coffee
$\frac{1}{2}$ oz butter
1 dessertspoon rum, or 2-3 drops vanilla essence
3 eggs
1 small carton (2$\frac{1}{2}$ fl oz) double cream

4-6 mousse, or custard pots

Method

Break the chocolate into small pieces, put into a pan with the liquid and stir continually over a gentle heat to a thick cream. The chocolate should be hot but the sides of the pan never so hot that you cannot touch them. Take off the heat, stir in the butter and flavouring.

Crack each of the eggs, putting the whites into the basin and dropping the yolks, one at a time, into the chocolate pan; stir well after each addition.

Watchpoint It is important that the chocolate is hot when the yolks go in so that they get slightly cooked.

Whisk the whites to a firm snow, then stir briskly into the chocolate. When thoroughly mixed fill the small pots and leave overnight in the larder or refrigerator. For easy pouring turn the mixture first into a jug, scraping the pan out well. These mousses may be served plain or a blob of cream can be spooned on to the top of each mousse, or piped with an 8-cut rose nozzle and forcing bag, preferably of nylon. Serve with cigarettes russes biscuits, see page 94.

Cigarettes russes biscuits

2 egg whites
4 oz caster sugar
2 oz butter
2 oz plain flour (sifted)
2-3 drops of vanilla essence

These biscuits are one of the many varieties of little cakes and sweetmeats (known as petits gâteaux and petits fours) which may be served with dishes such as ices or mousses, or on their own.

To shape cigarettes, roll each oblong tightly around a wooden spoon handle while biscuits are still warm

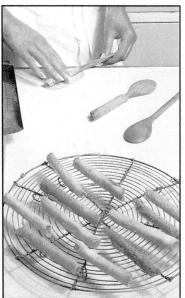

Method
Break up the egg whites in a basin, add the sugar and beat with a fork until smooth. Melt the butter and add with the sifted flour to the mixture. Flavour with 2-3 drops of vanilla essence.

Spread the mixture in oblongs on the greased and floured baking sheet and bake for 5-6 minutes in an oven at 400°F or Mark 6. (It is a good idea to test the mixture by baking one only at first. If difficult to handle, add a pinch of flour, or if too firm and hard, you can add 1 dessertspoon of melted butter.)

Take the oblongs out of the oven and allow to stand for 1-2 seconds, then remove them with a sharp knife, placing them upside down on the table. Roll each one tightly round a wooden spoon handle, skewer or pencil, holding it firmly with your hand. Remove at once from the spoon, and allow to cool. Store in an airtight tin.

Gâteaux and pastries

European gâteaux and pastries are in a class on their own. In the main centres — Vienna and France — they have been developed to an exquisite art, and the traditional names and decorations are carefully adhered to. Not that there is any lack of experiment with new decorations, but there are certain recipes which are instantly recognisable by their names.

English cakes and pastries are somewhat different from the French and Viennese, but the more ornamental are well qualified to appear beside their foreign kin in the pages of a recipe book.

This branch of cooking does require a certain amount of expertise, but with care and attention to detail you can get a professional looking, and tasting, result. French pâtisseries are usually based on pâte sucrée (French flan pastry), or on pâte à génoise commune (genoese pastry). Otherwise, bases are shortcrust, rich shortcrust and puff, pastries.

French flan pastry stands up better than shortcrust to being filled with fruit and glazed. It is made with plain flour, butter, caster sugar and egg yolks, and no liquid of any kind. The method of making (see recipe in Appendix) is completely different from English shortcrust pastry and, for this reason, the resulting paste should be firm and completely non-elastic. This means that the pastry keeps its shape during baking and when cooked is slightly short and melt-in-the-mouth. If using French flan pastry from the refrigerator, take it out 15-20 minutes before you use it and keep at room temperature.

You will see that the baking temperature for French flan pastry is a little lower than for English pastry, owing to its high proportion of sugar. When cooked it is a delicate biscuit colour — beware of overcooking it, though, as it becomes hard and tasteless.

For shaping the pastry, the traditional French tartlet mould is best if you are cooking French flan pastry. This is fairly deep and measures about 2-2$\frac{1}{2}$ inches in diameter. Most good ironmongers stock them. Otherwise an ordinary flan ring is often used, which allows you to remove the mould without disturbing the pastry.

Gâteaux are not always pastry-based; sometimes a cake mixture is used, usually sponge. Whatever the base, true gâteaux are a sure success at a party. They always look so delicious that no guest can resist them — and for the host or hostess there is the added advantage that all preparation can be completed well in advance.

Tartelettes coeur à la crème

For French flan pastry
4 oz plain flour
2 oz butter
2 oz caster sugar
2 egg yolks
2 drops of vanilla essence

For filling
4 oz Petit Suisse, or Demi-Sel,
  cream cheese
caster sugar (to taste)
2-3 tablespoons double cream
$\frac{1}{2}$ lb small ripe strawberries
  (hulled)
$\frac{1}{2}$ lb redcurrant jelly (see page 155)

6-8 tartlet tins

Method
Prepare pastry (see page 154) and chill for 1 hour before rolling out. Set oven at 350°F or Mark 5. Line tartlet tins with pastry, prick bottoms with a fork and bake blind for 8-10 minutes.

Rub the cream cheese through a small sieve, add sugar to taste and beat in the cream.

When the pastry cases are cold, fill with the cheese-cream mixture and cover with strawberries. Make a glaze from the redcurrant jelly by whisking until fairly smooth and rubbing through a strainer into a pan. Heat jelly gently without stirring until it is clear, then bring to the boil. Brush the warm glaze over the strawberries. Allow to set before serving.

Strawberry flan

For French flan pastry
4 oz plain flour
2 oz butter
2 oz caster sugar
2 egg yolks
2 drops of vanilla essence

For filling
$\frac{1}{2}$-$\frac{3}{4}$ lb strawberries
$\frac{1}{2}$ lb redcurrant jelly (see page 155)

6-inch diameter flan ring

Method
Prepare the pastry (see page 154) and chill for 1 hour before rolling out and lining the flan ring; bake blind in oven pre-set at 375°F or Mark 5 for 15-20 minutes.

Hull the strawberries. Prepare a redcurrant glaze (see method left).

When the flan case is cool, fill with the strawberries and brush with the hot glaze; allow it to set before serving.

Coeur à la crème. For the classic coeur à la crème, curd cheese is mixed with a little fresh double cream (plain or lightly whipped). This is then put into small wicker, heart-shaped baskets, lined with muslin, and left to drain for approximately 12 hours. When turned out, the little hearts are served with single cream poured over them, and sugared fruit.

Almond and raspberry flan

½ lb fresh raspberries

For almond pastry
3 oz butter
1 oz shortening
6 oz plain flour
1½ oz ground almonds
1½ oz caster sugar
2-3 drops of vanilla essence
1 large egg yolk, or 2 small egg yolks
1-2 tablespoons cold water

For almond meringue
3 small egg whites
6 oz caster sugar
6 oz ground almonds

For decoration
½ pint double cream
caster sugar (to taste)
2-3 drops of vanilla essence
browned, shredded almonds

8-inch diameter flan ring

Method
First prepare almond pastry: rub the fats into the flour, add the ground almonds and sugar. Mix the egg yolk(s) with vanilla essence and water and add to the dry ingredients. Work up lightly to a firm paste and chill for 15 minutes.

Set the oven at 350°F or Mark 4. Line the flan ring with the pastry, prick the bottom lightly and cover with the raspberries.

To prepare meringue: whip the egg whites until frothy, add the sugar a little at a time and continue whisking until the mixture stands in peaks. Fold in the ground almonds. Spread the almond mixture over the raspberries and bake in the preset moderate oven for about 30 minutes.

When the flan is cold, cover it with the cream, lightly sweetened, whipped and then flavoured with vanilla essence; decorate with the browned almonds.

Preparing almond and raspberry flan

Apricot flan

For rich shortcrust pastry
6 oz plain flour
pinch of salt
4½ oz butter
1 rounded dessertspoon granulated
sugar
1 egg yolk
2 tablespoons water

For filling
1 lb fresh apricots
½ pint water
3 oz granulated sugar
apricot glaze (see page 114)

7-8 inch diameter flan ring

Method
Make the rich shortcrust pastry (see page 156), set aside to chill.

Put the water and sugar into a shallow pan, dissolve on a slow heat, then boil rapidly for 2 minutes and draw aside.

Wash the apricots and cut in half with a serrated-edge, stainless steel knife, or fruit knife, by cutting down to, and round, the stone from the stalk end, following the slight groove on the side of the apricot. Give the fruit a twist to halve it. If the stones do not come away easily, poach the apricots whole. Once cooked the stones can be taken out without breaking the fruit. Some of the stones can be cracked, the kernels skinned and added to the fruit for special flavour.

Place the halved apricots in a pan, cut side uppermost, cover with syrup and heat gently to boiling point. This will draw out the juice and so increase the quantity of syrup, although this will not in the first instance cover the fruit. Simmer for about 15 minutes, or until the apricots are tender. Cool in the syrup.

Roll out the pastry, line on to the flan ring and bake blind. Cool on a pastry rack.

The prepared apricot glaze should be hot and well reduced. If too thin, reduce to a thicker consistency by boiling the liquid quickly in an uncovered pan. Brush a light coating of glaze over the bottom and sides of the flan. Lift the apricots from the syrup with a spoon and arrange in the flan. Brush well with the hot glaze.

Alternatively, the apricot syrup can be thickened with arrowroot and used instead of jam glaze. Jam is better, however, if the flan has to be kept for a while before serving.

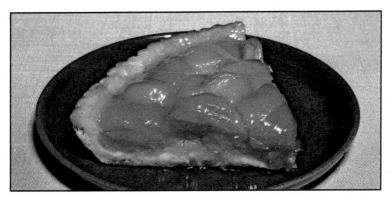

Cherry and praline flan

For French flan pastry
6 oz plain flour
pinch of salt
3 oz caster sugar
3 oz butter
3 egg yolks

For praline filling
2 oz unblanched almonds
2 oz caster sugar
1 tablespoon custard powder
¼ pint milk
¼ pint double cream (whipped)
1 teaspoon caster sugar

For topping
1 can pitted dark, or Morello, cherries
1 wineglass red wine
3-4 tablespoons redcurrant jelly (see page 155)
grated rind and juice of 1 orange

8-inch diameter flan ring

Almonds and burnt sugar being put through grater to make praline powder for the praline cream filling

Method

To prepare the pastry: sift the flour with the salt on to a pastry board or laminated-plastic work top. Make a well in the middle of the flour and add other ingredients. Work together with the finger-tips, knead until pastry is smooth; then chill for 30 minutes. Set oven at 375°F or Mark 5.

To make praline filling: heat almonds and sugar gently in a small heavy pan. When sugar is a liquid caramel, stir carefully with a metal spoon to toast nuts on all sides. Turn on to an oiled tin and leave to set. When cold, crush praline with a rolling pin or put through a nutmill, mincer or grater.

Mix the custard powder and milk to a paste in a saucepan and bring to the boil. Turn into a basin, whisk well and cover with wet greaseproof paper to prevent a skin from forming.

Roll out pastry, line on to flan ring and bake blind in pre-set oven for 12-15 minutes.

For topping: drain cherries. Boil wine to reduce it to half its quantity, add redcurrant jelly, orange rind and juice and heat gently until jelly has melted. Mix in cherries (keeping back a few to garnish the top) and leave to cool. When custard is cold, fold in whipped cream and praline, with caster sugar to taste. Fill pastry case with praline cream and spoon on cherry topping. Use the reserved cherries as decoration.

A rich cherry and praline flan makes ▶
an unusual cold sweet for a party

100

Praline is often used in confectionery, mixed with chocolate for rich fillings.

The origin of the name praline (for a sugared almond) dates from the time of Louis XIII. The Duc de Choiseul-Praslin was renowned for his conquests both in battle and the bedroom; he once offered his favourite mistress a new sweet (a sugared almond, in fact) which had such success that it was called *prasline,* and a confectionery shop was opened especially to sell it.

Rum pie

For shortcrust pastry
6 oz plain flour
3 oz butter
1 oz shortening
1 tablespoon caster sugar
1 egg yolk
1-2 tablespoons water

For filling
8 fl oz milk
$\frac{1}{4}$ nutmeg (grated)
2 eggs (separated)
3 oz caster sugar
pinch of salt
1 teaspoon gelatine (soaked in
    3 teaspoons cold water)
$\frac{1}{8}$ pint rum

To finish
1 oz plain chocolate
1 tablespoon water
$\frac{1}{4}$ pint double cream
1 teaspoon rum
1 dessertspoon caster sugar

7-8 inch diameter flan ring

Method
Prepare the shortcrust pastry
(see method, page 156). Line the
flan ring with it and bake blind
for 20-25 minutes, then set aside.

To prepare the filling: scald
the milk with the nutmeg. Beat
the egg yolks, sugar and salt together until thick and light in
colour, pour on the hot milk and
cook in a double saucepan until
the mixture coats the back of a
spoon. Stir in the soaked gelatine and allow to cool. When
the mixture begins to thicken,
stir in the rum and, finally, the
stiffly whisked egg whites. Pour
into the cooled pastry case
and put in the refrigerator to set.

Melt the chocolate in the
water, set pan aside and allow
it to cool. Whip the cream and
divide in half. Flavour half with
the rum and the other half with
the sugar. Mix the rum-flavoured
cream with the cold, melted
chocolate, cover the top of the
pie with the sugared cream and
then coat this with the chocolate cream. Chill to serve.

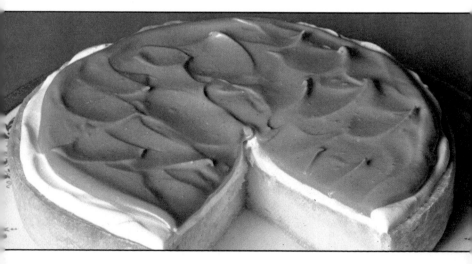

Strawberry tartlets

For rich shortcrust pastry
5 oz plain flour
pinch of salt
3 oz butter
1 teaspoon caster sugar
1 egg yolk
1½-2 tablespoons cold water

For filling
8 oz strawberries
redcurrant jelly glaze (see method,
    Tartelettes coeur à la crème,
    page 97)

Small tartlet tins

Method
Make the rich shortcrust pastry
(see method, page 156) and set
aside to chill. Line the pastry on
to the small tartlet tins and bake
blind (for about 8 minutes in an
oven at 375°F or Mark 5). Allow
to cool.

Hull (remove stalks from) the
strawberries and keep on one
side. Warm the redcurrant jelly
glaze but do not boil. Brush the
cases with the jelly, arrange
strawberries in the cases and
brush again with the glaze. The
amount of glaze should be
generous — sufficient to fill the
pastry cases and so hold strawberries firmly in place.

Tarte aux pommes à l'orange

(Apple and orange flan)

For French flan pastry
4 oz plain flour
2 oz caster sugar
2 egg yolks
2 oz butter
2-3 drops of vanilla essence

For filling
2 lb cooking apples (quartered,
  cored and sliced)
3-4 tablespoons granulated sugar
grated rind of 2 oranges

To finish
2 seedless oranges (sliced in
  rounds)
3-4 tablespoons apricot glaze (see
page 114)

7-8 inch diameter flan ring

Method

First prepare pastry (see method, page 154). Chill pastry in refrigerator for at least 30 minutes.

Set oven at 375°F or Mark 5. Roll out pastry and line flan ring. Bake blind in pre-set oven for 15 minutes.

Meanwhile prepare filling: slice apples into a buttered pan, cover with a tight-fitting lid and cook to a pulp. Rub through a strainer and return purée to the pan with sugar and orange rind. Cook until thick, stirring all the time. Turn out and cool a little.

Fill the flan case with the apple purée and smooth over the top. Cut peel and pith from the oranges, slice into rounds and arrange on top of the flan. Brush the oranges with warm glaze (jam dissolved in a little water and lemon juice, sieved, then boiled until clear). Leave to set; serve flan cold.

1 *For French flan pastry make well in flour, put in sugar, yolks, butter and vanilla*
2 *Then, with fingertips of one hand only, work all these added ingredients to a paste*

3 *Draw in flour quickly, kneading lightly until smooth; remember to chill pastry well before you use it*

Peach croissants with iced zabaione

3-4 peaches
caster sugar
6 croissants
1 oz butter

For zabaione
2 oz sugar
1 tablespoon water
1 egg white
3 egg yolks
1 tablespoon Marsala, or golden
   sherry

Method

Peel, stone and slice peaches.
Place slices in an airtight container, layered with sugar; when
container is full, seal it and
place upside-down in refrigerator for at least 2 hours.

To make the zabaione, put the
sugar and water into a small
pan and dissolve the sugar
slowly over low heat; then boil
up quickly to 250°-260°F, or
until a little of the syrup will
form a hard ball when dropped
into cold water. Beat the egg
white until stiff, add the sugar
syrup and mix quickly with a
whisk until thick. Place the egg
yolks and Marsala (or sherry)
into a bowl and whisk over a pan
of hot water until thick and
mousse-like; combine with the
meringue mixture and chill
thoroughly. Melt the butter in a
frying pan, add about 2-3 tablespoons of the syrup from the
peaches and allow to bubble
together for 2-3 minutes. Fry the
croissants in this mixture until
golden-brown, remove from the
pan, arrange around a serving
dish, keep warm. Put chilled
peaches and syrup in the middle
of the dish of croissants and
pour over the zabaione.

*Frying the croissants in butter and
the syrup from the chilled peaches*

*Piling chilled peach slices into the
centre of the dish of fried croissants*

*Combining the meringue and mousse
mixtures to make the zabaione*

Galette normande

For Danish shortcrust pastry
8 oz plain flour
6 oz butter
2½ oz icing sugar
2 egg yolks
2-3 drops of vanilla essence

For apple marmelade
2½ lb cooking apples
½ oz butter
grated rind of ½ lemon
4-6 oz granulated sugar

For icing
4 rounded tablespoons icing
    sugar (sifted)
2-3 tablespoons sugar syrup
1-2 drops of vanilla essence
2 tablespoons redcurrant jelly
    (see page 155) — well beaten

Paper forcing bag

Method

First prepare Danish shortcrust pastry : sift flour on to your work surface, make a well in the centre and put in butter, icing sugar, egg yolks and vanilla essence. Work the mixture to a smooth paste with your hand, then chill for at least 1 hour before using.

Meanwhile prepare apple marmelade. Wipe, quarter and core the apples ; slice them into a pan, rubbed around with butter, then cover with well-buttered paper and a lid, and cook apples gently to a pulp. Rub this pulp through a fine sieve, then return the purée to the pan with the lemon rind and sugar. Boil rapidly until marmelade is really thick, stirring frequently ; turn it into a flat dish to cool.

Sandwiching shortcrust pastry rounds and apple marmelade for galette

Feathering the icing and redcurrant jelly with the point of a knife

Divide the pastry into three, roll out each piece into a round, 8 inches in diameter. Slide these on to baking sheets, prick pastry with a fork and bake in the oven, pre-set at 375°F or Mark 5, for 10-12 minutes, or until a pale, biscuit colour. Leave rounds to cool.

Sandwich the rounds together with apple marmelade. Mix the icing sugar with the sugar syrup and vanilla essence until it is a thick cream. Heat this gently, then coat the galette. Decorate at once with redcurrant jelly, using the paper forcing bag to pipe it in lines on to the cake. Then draw a skewer or the point of a knife across the jelly lines in alternate directions to 'feather' decoration.

Apple slice

8 oz plain flour (sifted with a
  pinch of salt)
3 oz white cooking fat
squeeze of lemon juice
about ¼ pint iced water
3 oz butter

For filling
1 lb cooking apples (peeled,
  cored and sliced)
1 oz candied peel (finely
  chopped)
1½ oz sultanas
½ teaspoon cinnamon

To glaze
1 egg white, or 1 egg (beaten)
caster sugar
½ oz almonds (blanched and
  halved)

To finish
2 tablespoons apricot glaze (see
  page 114)

Method

Rub half of the cooking fat into
the sifted flour. Add the lemon
juice to the iced water and use
this to mix flour to a soft dough.

Roll out an oblong three times
as long as it is wide. Using half
the butter, place small pats of
butter over two-thirds of the
dough and fold in three, placing
plain third against dough with
fat. Seal the edges lightly
and chill. Give a quarter-turn
and repeat the process first with
the remaining cooking fat and
then the butter, chilling well
between each roll and fold. Roll
and fold once more (without
fat) and chill again.

Now prepare the filling by
mixing all the filling ingredients
together.

Roll pastry thinly to an oblong
approximately 14 by 10 inches
and divide unequally into two
pieces about 14 by 4½ inches
and 14 by 5½ inches. Place the
smaller piece on a baking tray
and, leaving a 1-inch clear edge
of pastry, put filling down the
centre, piling it up well. Fold
the second piece of pastry in
half lengthways. With a sharp
knife, make cuts through the
two layers — at right angles to
the fold and at 1-inch intervals
— not quite to the open edge.
Dampen the edges of the first
piece of pastry and open out
the slit piece. Place it on the
fruit filling, with the cuts gaping
slightly, and seal the edges.
Set the oven at 425°F or Mark 7,
and chill the apple slice for 10
minutes.

Glaze the top with egg white
(or beaten egg), scatter over
the nuts and sprinkle with
sugar. Bake at the top of the
pre-set oven for 20 minutes.
Then reduce the heat to 375°F
or Mark 5 for 10-15 minutes
until golden and crisp. Remove
to a cooling rack and brush
lightly with hot apricot glaze.

*The slit piece of pastry is laid over
apple filling and the edges sealed*

Pineapple curd cake

For pastry
4 oz plain flour
pinch of salt
1 teaspoon granulated sugar
2 oz butter
½ oz shortening
1 tablespoon distilled white
vinegar
1 tablespoon milk

For filling
1 small pineapple, or ½ a large one
8 oz Philadelphia, or curd, cheese
2 tablespoons granulated sugar
2 egg yolks
¼ pint double cream

7-8 inch diameter flan ring

Method
Prepare the pastry. Sift flour with salt and sugar, rub in fats, and mix to a firm dough with the vinegar and milk. Roll out to a round the same diameter as the flan ring, and fit the pastry into the ring's base. Prick lightly and set aside.

Set oven at 375°F or Mark 5.

Beat the cheese until smooth, add the sugar, egg yolks and cream. Turn the mixture into the ring and bake in the pre-set oven for 20-30 minutes until firm to the touch.

In the meantime, cut the skin from the pineapple, cut flesh into slices and core them, dust slices with sugar. When curd cake is cooked, leave it until cold, and then arrange the pineapple on top, slightly overlapping the slices. Serve with a bowl of lightly whipped cream.

Mixing sugar, egg yolks and cream with beaten cheese to make curd cake

Overlapping fresh pineapple slices on top of cooked and cooled cake

Pineapple cake

1 fresh pineapple (sliced and diced) and 2-3 tablespoons caster sugar, or 1 large can pineapple slices
1 tablespoon kirsch

For sponge
3 eggs
4½ oz caster sugar
3 oz plain flour
pinch of salt

To decorate
¼-½ pint double cream
6-8 tablespoons apricot glaze (see page 114)
strip of angelica cut into 8-10 diamond shapes

9-inch diameter sandwich tin

Method
If using a fresh pineapple, remove the skin, cut in even slices (about ¼ inch deep) and stamp out the core with a small cutter. Take the smaller slices from the top and bottom and cut into dice. Sprinkle both the slices and dice with the sugar and kirsch and leave for at least 1 hour.

If using canned pineapple and the slices are very thick, drain and divide them. Dice about two slices and sprinkle both dice and slices with kirsch. No extra sugar is needed for canned pineapple.

To make sponge: set oven at

If whisking by hand, place the basin over a half-full saucepan of boiling water, so that the gentle heat dissolves the sugar and obtains volume from the beaten eggs. The batter is ready when it falls from the whisk in a thick ribbon and holds its shape

350°F or Mark 4. Prepare sandwich tin: brush or smooth a thin layer of butter on the bottom of the tin and line with a disc of greaseproof paper. Grease the paper and sides of the tin and dust first with caster sugar and then with flour; tap the tin to shake out any surplus. Break the eggs into the bowl and slowly stir in the sugar. If whisking by hand, have ready a saucepan half-full of boiling water on which your mixing bowl or basin will sit without touching the water. This heat is necessary to get the greatest volume from the eggs and to dissolve sugar. Remove the pan of water from the stove, sit the mixing bowl on top and whisk the mixture over this gentle heat until it thickens and becomes mousse-like; this will take some 7-8 ▶

Pineapple cake
continued

minutes. The batter is ready when a little lifted on the whisk falls in a thick ribbon on mixture in the bowl and holds its shape.

Remove the bowl from the heat and continue whisking until the mixture is cold. If using an electric beater, no heat is needed; just whisk for a longer time. Sift the flour with the salt and, using a metal spoon, fold it into the mixture quickly and lightly. Turn this into the prepared tin and bake for 15-20 minutes in the pre-set oven. Cool on a wire rack.

Whip the cream until thick and flavour with a little of the kirsch from the pineapple. Split the sponge cake in half and fill with cream and diced pineapple. Brush top with hot apricot glaze, and when set arrange pineapple slices overlapping to cover the top; brush again with hot apricot glaze and decorate cake with diamonds of angelica.

Apricot glaze

This can be made in large quantities at a time, as it keeps well in a covered jar.

To make 1 lb of glaze: turn 1 lb of apricot jam into a saucepan and add the juice from $\frac{1}{2}$ a lemon and 4 tablespoons water. Bring slowly to the boil, then simmer for 5 minutes. If glaze is to be kept, strain, return to pan and boil for a further 5 minutes before cooling and putting into a jam jar.

To use immediately, continue boiling until the mixture is thick, then brush generously over the fruit. If using a smooth jam (with no lumps of fruit) water is not needed.

Apricot curd cake

$\frac{1}{2}$ lb apricots (stoned)
sugar syrup (made with $\frac{1}{3}$ pint water and 2 tablespoons granulated sugar)
6 oz sweet biscuits (eg. Nice)
2 oz butter
1 lb curd cheese
4 oz caster sugar
1 large, or 2 small, eggs (well beaten)
2-3 drops of vanilla essence
cream (lightly whipped)

7-inch diameter loose-bottomed flan, or sandwich, tin

Method
Set oven at 350°F or Mark 4. Make sugar syrup and poach apricots (see page 15). Crush biscuits with a rolling pin; rub $\frac{1}{2}$ oz butter over bottom and sides of the flan tin.

Rub the curd cheese through a wire strainer. Cream rest of butter, add sugar and cheese by degrees with the egg and beat until light and fluffy; flavour with vanilla essence. Scatter half biscuit crumbs over bottom and sides of tin, then carefully spoon in curd mixture. Smooth top with a palette knife, scatter over remaining crumbs. Bake in pre-set oven 25-30 minutes.

Leave overnight, or at least 4 hours, before removing from tin. Drain apricots, arrange over top of cake; boil syrup until thick, spoon over apricots. Serve with whipped cream.

Strawberry walnut cream cake

3 eggs
scant 4 oz sugar
3 oz plain flour
2 oz walnuts (coarsely chopped)
2 tablespoons coffee essence

For filling
8-10 fl oz double cream (lightly
  whipped)
1 lb strawberries

Deep 8-inch diameter cake tin

Method
Prepare the tin by greasing and dusting out with caster sugar and flour. Set the oven at 350°F or Mark 4.

To prepare the cake mixture : whisk the eggs and sugar over heat as for a whisked sponge (see method, page 113), or combine using an electric mixer (without heat). When really thick and mousse-like, take off the heat and continue to whisk for a further minute. Sift the flour and fold it in with the walnuts and coffee essence. Turn the cake mixture into the tin and bake in pre-set oven for 40-45 minutes.

Turn cake out to cool and when cold split into three and layer with two-thirds of the lightly whipped cream mixed with the sliced strawberries. (Reserve a few strawberries for decoration.) The filling should be really lavish. Spread the rest of the cream over the top of the cake and decorate with the reserved strawberries.

Angel cake with strawberries in muscat syrup

2 oz plain flour
6½ oz caster sugar
6 egg whites
pinch of salt
¾ teaspoon cream of tartar
3 drops of vanilla essence
2 drops of almond essence

To finish
¾ pint double cream
1 teaspoon caster sugar
2-3 drops of vanilla essence
1 lb strawberries
¼ pint muscat syrup (see right)

8-9 inch diameter angel cake tin (with funnelled base)

Method

Set the oven at 375°F or Mark 5.

Sift the flour and 3½ oz of the caster sugar three times and set aside.

Place the egg whites, salt and cream of tartar in a large dry pudding basin and whisk with a rotary beater until mixture is foamy. Add remaining 3 oz of sugar, 2 tablespoons at a time, and the essences and continue beating until the mixture will stand in peaks. Carefully fold in the sifted flour and sugar.

Turn the mixture into the clean dry cake tin, level the surface and draw a knife through the mixture to break any air bubbles. Bake the cake in pre-set hot oven for 30-35 minutes or until no imprint remains when you lightly touch the top with your finger.

When the cake is done, turn it upside down on a wire rack and leave until quite cold; it will then fall easily from the tin. Cut cake in three layers with a serrated-edge knife.

Drawing a knife through the cake mixture to break up any air bubbles

After layering and masking the cake with cream, pipe rosettes on top

Watchpoint A serrated-edge knife is important as the cake's texture is very delicate. Use a sawing movement for best results.

Lightly whip the cream, then add the sugar and vanilla essence and continue whisking until thick. Spread each layer with cream, re-shape cake and mask with the whipped cream. Decorate the top and outside edge of the cake with rosettes of cream and strawberries.

Hull the remaining strawberries and cut in thick slices. Spoon muscat syrup over them; serve separately in a bowl.

Muscat syrup

3 lb gooseberries
$\frac{1}{2}$ pint water
$2\frac{3}{4}$ lb lump sugar
8 large elderflowers

Method

Wash, top and tail gooseberries, put in a pan with the water and simmer until they are soft. Add sugar, dissolve over gentle heat and bring to the boil. Tie elderflowers in a piece of muslin and add to syrup. Draw pan aside and leave to infuse for 7-10 minutes. Strain syrup through muslin. Use as required, pour remainder into screwtop jars for storing.

Strawberry shortcake

8 oz plain flour
5 oz butter
2½ oz icing sugar
2 egg yolks
4-6 drops of vanilla essence
1 lb strawberries (hulled)
½ pint double cream
caster sugar (to taste)
icing sugar

Method

First sift the flour on to your working surface, make a well in the centre and put in the butter, icing sugar, egg yolks and 2-3 drops of vanilla essence. Work these ingredients to a smooth paste, then set the mixture in a cool place for 1 hour before using.

Set oven at 350°F or Mark 4.

Divide the pastry in two, roll or pat out into two 9-inch rounds, ¼ inch thick, place on a baking sheet and bake in the pre-set oven for 15-20 minutes. Trim shortcake while still warm and cut one round into eight sections. Cool on a wire rack.

Slice the strawberries, reserving eight whole ones for decoration. Whip the cream, sweeten to taste, and add 2-3 drops of vanilla essence; put one-third of the cream aside for decoration. Mix the sliced strawberries into the remainder of the cream.

Put the cream and fruit on the plain round of shortcake, smooth over and arrange the sections of shortcake on the top. Dust with icing sugar and decorate with rosettes of cream and reserved strawberries.

Gâteau Margot

4 oz plain flour
4 eggs
6 oz caster sugar
pinch of salt

For filling
1 lb strawberries (or 2 packets of frozen ones)
1 tablespoon caster sugar
4 oz plain block chocolate
½ pint double cream
vanilla essence

Ring mould (3 pints capacity)

This quantity serves 12 people.

Method

Set oven at 375°F or Mark 5. Grease, sugar and flour the tin or mould. Sift the flour with the salt and set aside. Whisk the eggs and sugar together over hot water until thick and mousse-like (no heat is necessary if an electric mixer is used). Remove the bowl from the heat and continue beating until the mixture is cold; fold in flour with a metal spoon and turn at once into the prepared tin. Bake in the pre-set oven for about 35-40 minutes; then turn on to a wire rack to cool.

Meanwhile, take about one-third of the strawberries, cut in thick slices, sprinkle with caster sugar and leave for 10-15 minutes, then rub them through a nylon strainer to make a purée. Grate the chocolate on to a plate; place over a pan of hot water to melt.

Cut the cake across in three rounds, spread each layer with a thin coating of chocolate and leave to set. Whip the cream until thick, take about one-third and flavour with the strawberry purée. Spread this over the layers and sandwich them to-gether. Sweeten and flavour the remaining cream with vanilla and spread over the cake with a palette knife. Pile remaining strawberries in middle.

Left : spreading the whipped cream and strawberry purée on to the rounds of cake for gâteau Margot. These have already been coated with a thin layer of chocolate

Right : spreading the whipped cream over cake after it has been sandwiched together

Danish raspberry shortcake

1 lb raspberries (frozen, or fresh in season)
3 tablespoons redcurrant glaze (see method, Tartelettes coeur à la crème, page 97)
1 small carton (about 3 fl oz) double cream (whipped) — optional

For pastry
4 oz plain flour
3 oz butter
1¼ oz icing sugar (sifted)
1 egg yolk
2-3 drops of vanilla essence

We have found that if you buy raspberries frozen without sugar, which are packed in a rigid container, and leave them to thaw overnight at refrigerator temperature, they will be quite dry and will look and taste like the freshly-picked fruit. If you cannot find these, you should use a firmer fruit such as pineapple or apricots with an apricot glaze. Do not use canned raspberries as they are too soft to glaze.

Method
First prepare pastry : sift the flour on to a board or marble slab, make a well in the middle and put all the other ingredients in this. Work them to a smooth paste with the fingertips of one hand, drawing in the flour gradually ; then chill pastry in refrigerator for 30 minutes.

Meanwhile set oven at 375°F or Mark 5.

Roll or pat out pastry to a round, ¼ inch thick and 7-8 inches in diameter, slide it on to a baking sheet and bake blind in preset oven for about 15-20 minutes. The pastry should not brown but look like shortbread.

When pastry is cool, cover it' with the raspberries and brush with redcurrant glaze. When quite cold, decorate shortcake with whipped cream or serve it separately.

Watchpoint If you choose a canned fruit, it is wise to make double the quantity of glaze and brush the shortcake with a thin coating of this, then leave it to set before arranging drained fruit on top. This will prevent juices from the canned fruit on top soaking into the pastry. Glaze a second time on top of the fruit.

Brush the glaze thickly over the raspberries and leave it to set, then decorate or serve cream separately

Whip the cream and use a forcing bag and vegetable rose nozzle to pipe round this attractive border

Gâteau chinois à l'orange

4 oz plain flour
pinch of salt
4 eggs
6 oz caster sugar
5-6 sugar lumps
2 oranges
¾ pint double cream
2-3 tablespoons sliced glacé
   ginger

For decoration
extra double cream
extra glacé ginger, or crystallised orange slices

2-6 baking sheets ; 2-6 cooling racks

Method

Prepare the baking sheets in the following way: brush with melted lard or oil, dust lightly with flour, then mark an 8-inch circle on each, using a plate or saucepan lid as a guide. Set the oven at 375°F or Mark 5.

Sift the flour with the salt. Break the eggs into a bowl, add the sugar and whisk over hot water until the mixture is thick and white (if using electric mixer, no heat is necessary). Remove from the heat and continue whisking until the bowl is cold. Fold the flour lightly into the mixture, using a metal spoon. Divide mixture into 6 portions and spread each over a circle on the prepared sheets (this can be done with fewer sheets, in rotation, but each time they must be wiped, regreased and floured). Bake in the pre-set moderate oven for about 5-8 minutes. Trim each round with a sharp knife while still on the baking sheet, then lift it on to a wire rack to cool.

Rub the sugar lumps over the oranges to remove all the zest, then pound sugar to a syrup with a little orange juice. Whip the cream and sweeten with the orange syrup. Sandwich the 6 rounds of cake with the orange cream and sliced ginger. Decorate with extra cream, and ginger or crystallised orange slices.

Gâteau allemande with raspberries

4 eggs (separated)
7 oz caster sugar
3½ oz ground almonds
grated rind and juice of ½ lemon
3½ oz fine semolina
8 oz lemon-flavoured glacé
   icing (see page 154)

To serve
1-1½ lb raspberries
caster sugar (to taste)

Deep 9-inch diameter cake tin

Method
Set the oven at 375°F or Mark 5 and prepare cake tin : grease it, put a disc of paper at bottom, sugar and flour it. Beat the egg yolks and sugar together until thick and white. Work in the ground almonds and the grated rind and juice of the lemon and leave the mixture to stand for 3 minutes.

Whisk the egg whites until stiff, fold them into the mixture with the semolina, then turn it into the prepared tin and bake in the pre-set oven for about 50 minutes. When the cake is cool, coat it with the icing. Sprinkle the raspberries with sugar and serve separately.

Gâteau Bigarreau

1½ lb whiteheart cherries

For cake
3 eggs
4½ oz caster sugar
3 oz plain flour (well sifted
   with a pinch of salt)

For filling
good ¼ pint double cream (lightly whipped), or pastry cream (see method, Strawberry tabatières, page 12)
2 tablespoons praline (see page 100)

For glaze
3 tablespoons apricot jam
3 tablespoons redcurrant jelly (see page 155)
1-2 tablespoons water

For decoration
extra praline, or almonds
   (browned and chopped)

Shallow 8-inch diameter cake tin

Method
Set oven at 350°F or Mark 4. Grease tin, put a disc of paper at bottom, sugar and flour it.

Break eggs into a bowl and whisk in sugar gradually. Stand bowl over a pan of hot water or use an electric mixer (without heat) and whisk steadily until mixture is white and thick. Fold in flour and turn mixture into prepared tin. Bake in pre-set oven for 25-30 minutes.

Stone the cherries. Put the jam, jelly and water into a pan, simmer gently until smooth, then strain and cool. Fold praline into the whipped, or pastry, cream.

When cake is cool, split in two and sandwich with praline cream. Brush top with glaze and cover with cherries ; brush again thickly with warm glaze. Press praline (or almonds) round sides.

Gâteau pistache

3 eggs
3¾ oz sugar
2¾ oz flour
1 oz butter
6 oz quantity butter cream (see
    page 152)
1 oz pistachio nuts
    (blanched and pounded to a paste)
apricot glaze (see page 114)
few whole pistachio nuts (to
    decorate)

For glacé icing
12 oz icing sugar
sugar syrup (to moisten)
1 tablespoon kirsch (to flavour)

*Deep 8-inch diameter cake tin, or
    moule à manqué*

Method
Set oven at 350°F or Mark 4.
Prepare tin by brushing with
melted butter, lining with greaseproof paper, re-brushing with fat
and dusting with flour.

To make sponge : put the
eggs into a basin with the
sugar ; stand this basin in
another one containing very
hot water and whisk steadily
until the mixture is white and
thick. Fold flour into the mixture
with a metal spoon, then the
well softened butter. Turn the
mixture into tin and bake in
a pre-set moderate oven for
30-35 minutes, or until the cake
comes away from the side of the
tin. Turn it out on to a rack to
cool.

Flavour butter cream with the
pistachio paste.

Split cake in two, sandwich
halves with butter cream. Brush
the cake with warm apricot
glaze. Make the glacé icing (see
page 154). Add the kirsch and
warm to 100°F. Ice cake ; decorate with whole pistachio nuts.

Chocolate and strawberry gâteau

about 12 oz plain block chocolate
¾ lb strawberries (hulled)
¼ pint stock syrup — see right
    (flavoured with vanilla, or rum, or
    sherry)
½ pint double cream (lightly
    whipped)

For sponge
1 egg
2 oz caster sugar
1½ oz plain flour
pinch of salt

*6-7 inch diameter sandwich tin (2
    inches deep) and 8-9 inch dia-
    meter sandwich tin*

Method
First grease, sugar and flour the
smaller tin.

Break up the chocolate, put it
on a plate and set it over a pan
of hot water to melt. Then
remove, and work it well with a
palette knife until thick enough
to spread.

Line the large cake tin with
foil, then spread the inside and
bottom of the case fairly thickly
with chocolate, using the back
of a spoon. Make sure the sides
are well coated, then leave it
to set for several hours.

Meanwhile prepare and bake

*Spreading chocolate over the foil
to make the outer case of the gâteau*

the sponge (see method, page 113), using the small tin.

Carefully peel off foil from chocolate case. The easiest way to do this is as follows : lift the case out of the tin and start to peel and bend the foil outwards, away from the chocolate. Continue in this way until much of the sides and bottom are free, always keeping your hand on the outside of the foil to avoid touching the chocolate. Lastly, slide the case on to a wire rack and detach the last piece of foil.

Split the sponge cake in two, lay one round in the chocolate case and spoon over sufficient cold stock syrup (about half) to soak it well.

Slice the hulled strawberries, reserving a few for decoration.

Moisten them with 1-2 tablespoons of stock syrup and put them on top of the sponge. Cover them with a layer of cream, then the other round of sponge and spoon over the rest of the syrup. Pile the remaining cream on top and decorate with reserved strawberries.

Stock syrup : put 8 oz sugar and $\frac{1}{4}$ pint water in a pan and heat gently until sugar is dissolved. Then bring to boil and boil steadily for 10 minutes (220°F on a sugar thermometer). Allow to cool and store in a screw-top jar. This will give more than $\frac{1}{2}$ pint syrup.

Chocolate and strawberry gâteau, with its outer chocolate case

Peach and hazelnut galette

4-5 peaches
2-3 oz plain block chocolate
½ pint double cream
1 teaspoon caster sugar
2-3 drops of vanilla essence
2 oz icing sugar (sifted)

For galette
5 egg whites
7 oz caster sugar
2 oz hazelnuts (ground and
    browned)
3 oz shelled walnuts (ground)
3 oz plain flour (sifted)
2 oz butter

Method

Take four sheets of non-stick kitchen paper and draw an 8-inch diameter circle on each. Set oven at 350°F or Mark 4.

First make the galette: whisk the egg whites until stiff and dry, then fold in the sugar, prepared nuts and flour. Soften the butter in a small, warm basin until it will pour but is not oily, then fold this into the mixture. Spread the mixture thinly over the circles marked on the paper, slide them on to baking sheets and bake in pre-set moderate oven for about 30 minutes or until pale golden-brown. To achieve an even colour, turn the baking sheets around from time to time. When ready, remove the paper and cool each galette on a wire rack. (The cooking can be done in two batches, if you are short of baking sheets.)

Meanwhile grate the chocolate, or cut it finely, put it on a flame-proof plate and melt very slowly over a pan of hot water, or on top of the stove. Work with a palette knife until smooth, but do not allow it to become more than hand-hot. Spread chocolate

Above : spreading melted chocolate on to rounds of greaseproof paper for chocolate discs

Below : sandwiching the peaches and cream in between the galette rounds

126

evenly over a sheet of foil or greaseproof paper (just enough to coat), leave in a cool place and, when nearly set, cut into 15-20 circles with a $1\frac{1}{2}$-inch diameter pastry cutter. Leave to set firmly, then peel off the foil, or cut the circles before spreading on the chocolate (see left).

Whip the cream until thick, add the sugar and vanilla essence and continue beating until the cream stands in peaks.

Scald and skin the peaches, remove stones, slice flesh and mix with the cream. Sandwich galette rounds with peaches and cream, dust top with icing sugar and press chocolate rounds on to the sides, using a little reserved cream to make them stick.

Gâteau mille feuilles au citron

8 oz quantity of puff pastry (see
  page 155)
¾ pint double cream
5-6 oz apricot glaze (see page 114)

For lemon curd filling (see note)
8 oz caster sugar
4 oz unsalted butter
grated rind and juice of 2 large
  lemons
3 eggs (well beaten)

For decoration
small shapes made from
  trimmings of puff pastry
crystallised fruits
almonds, or pistachio nuts

4-5 inch diameter plain cutter

Note : you will need only about
a third of this lemon curd mixture
for gâteau mille feuilles au
citron, but make the full quantity
and the remainder will store for
several weeks in a cool place.

Method
Set oven at 400°F or Mark 6,
and dampen a baking sheet.

Roll out pastry very thinly and
cut 2 rounds the size of a
dessert plate ; remove the
centres of each round with the
cutter to leave a large ring of
pastry. From remaining pastry
cut a plain circle, a little thicker
and larger than the rings, to
form base for the cake.

Place the pastry rings on the
baking sheet, prick them well
with a fork and bake in pre-set
hot oven for 8 minutes. Then
prick and bake the circles on a
dampened baking sheet for
12-15 minutes. Make any pastry
trimmings into tiny stars, diamonds, etc., bake in the hot
oven for 5-7 minutes, or until
brown, then leave to cool.

Put all the ingredients for
lemon curd into an enamel pan
or stone jam jar standing in
boiling water. Stir gently over
low heat until mixture is thick.
(It must not boil or it will curdle.)
Pour into a bowl and allow to
cool.

When all the pastry is cool,
brush with warm apricot glaze
and mount one ring on top of
another on a base. The gâteau
has one plain circle as a base
and two rings. Brush the top
and sides with apricot glaze
and decorate with the small
pastry shapes, crystallised fruit
or chopped nuts.

To serve : reserve a little
cream for decoration and whip
the remainder until it begins to
thicken, then fold in the lemon
curd. Fill the gâteau with curd
mixture and decorate the top
with rosettes of whipped cream,
crystallised fruit and chopped
nuts.

*Decorating gâteau mille feuilles with
pastry shapes and crystallised fruit*

Creams

Smooth, silky, creamy, milky — simple creams that take not a thought to eat and are equally delicious whatever the weather. Children love them, and adults can't resist them even after the richest dinner.

It is eggs that give these cream desserts their velvety consistency. Usually whole eggs are used, with extra egg yolks added. Sometimes whipped egg whites add to the lightness of texture, and sometimes partially whipped cream, folded into the custard base, will increase the richness.

With eggs and milk the main

129

ingredients of these delicous sweets, they are as nourishing to eat as they are tempting to look at.

When making the soft custard base, it is important that it is absolutely smooth. Scald the milk then thicken the custard very, very gently indeed. It is probably easiest to use a double saucepan, the lower pan containing hot water; but if you are extremely careful it is possible to thicken your base over direct, but gentle, heat. You will also find it better to strain a custard base to remove any 'strings' of white that may not have completely blended with the sauce.

Crème florentine

¾ pint milk
4 egg yolks
1½ oz caster sugar
½ oz gelatine (soaked in 4
  tablespoons cold water)
½ pint double cream (lightly
  whipped)

For almond praline
2 oz almonds (unblanched)
2 oz caster sugar

To finish
1 fresh pineapple, or 1 large can
  pineapple slices
4 tablespoons caster sugar (for
  fresh pineapple)
1 miniature bottle of kirsch
  (optional)

*Fluted sponge cake mould (1½ pints
  capacity) ; enamel plate, or baking
  sheet*

Method

Lightly oil the cake mould and plate or baking sheet.

To prepare almond praline : put the almonds with 2 oz caster sugar in a small, heavy pan over gentle heat. As the sugar begins to change colour, increase the heat a little and stir carefully with a metal spoon, turning the almonds to make sure they get toasted right through. When the mixture is a rich brown caramel, tip it quickly on to the plate or baking sheet. Leave it to cool, then crush with a rolling pin or pass through a mincer or nut mill. Set aside.

Scald the milk, cream the egg yolks and remaining sugar together until thick and light in colour, then pour on the hot milk. Return mixture to the saucepan and stir continually over very gentle heat until the custard coats the back of a wooden spoon. (A double saucepan may be used.)

Strain the custard into a bowl, add the soaked gelatine and stir until it is dissolved ; leave to cool. Stand the bowl of custard in cold water, with ice cubes added, and gently stir the custard until it begins to thicken. Then fold in the cream and almond praline. Turn the mousse into the prepared mould, cover with foil and leave in the refrigerator to set.

Meanwhile remove the skin from the fresh pineapple, cut flesh in slices and remove the core. Dust with sugar and sprinkle with the kirsch. Turn out the mousse and surround with the pineapple slices.

Brown bread cream with damson sauce

3 slices wholemeal bread (2-3
days old)
1 tablespoon caster sugar
¾ pint milk
pared rind and juice of ½ lemon
3 egg yolks
1½ oz caster sugar
5 tablespoons water
½ oz gelatine
¼ pint double cream
½ lb damsons
½ pint water
4 tablespoons granulated sugar

*Decorative mould, or glass bowl
(1¼-1½ pints capacity)*

*Left : crumbs of stale wholemeal
bread are dusted with sugar before
being browned in the oven*
*Right : when the chilled custard,
with cream added, is on the point
of setting, the crisp browned breadcrumbs are folded quickly into it*

Method

After removing crusts, rub the
bread through a wire sieve or
reduce to crumbs a little at a
time in a liquidiser. Set the
oven at 350°F or Mark 4. Spread
out the crumbs on a sheet of
greaseproof paper on a baking
sheet, dust with the sugar and
put in the pre-set moderate
oven to brown. Allow to cool.

Watchpoint Great care must be
taken to brown the crumbs as
evenly as possible, so turn them
with a fork several times while
they are browning. The time the
crumbs take to brown will
depend on the freshness of the
bread, but allow 10 minutes —
they must be very crisp.

Heat the milk with the lemon
rind to scalding point, cover
and leave to infuse. Lightly oil
the mould, or have ready the
glass bowl. Work the egg yolks
and sugar together with a
wooden spoon until thick and
light in colour, strain on the hot
milk. Pour the water and lemon
juice on to the gelatine and
leave soaking. Return the egg

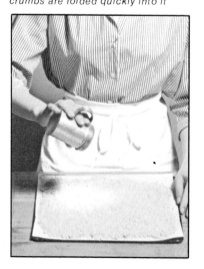

and milk mixture to the rinsed saucepan and stir briskly over heat until it thickens and coats the back of the wooden spoon. Strain quickly into a large bowl, add the soaked gelatine, stir until dissolved and then leave to cool, but not in a refrigerator.

When the custard is quite cold, tip it into a thin saucepan. Lightly whip the cream and fold it into the custard. Stand the saucepan in a bowl of cold water with a few ice cubes added. Stir gently until the custard is on the point of setting, then quickly fold in the crisp brown breadcrumbs. Pour it into the prepared mould or glass bowl, cover and leave in the refrigerator, or in a cool place, for 1-2 hours to set.

Cook the damsons with the water and sugar until soft and pulpy, then rub through a strainer. (Damson jelly, or home-made damson cheese (see page 22) can also be used; just melt it in a saucepan over heat with 2-3 tablespoons of water, then cool.) To serve, turn cream out of the mould and pour the damson sauce over or around it. Or serve from the glass bowl, decorated with extra cream, and hand sauce separately.

Redcurrant cream

1½ lb redcurrants
caster sugar (to taste)
2 egg yolks
1 egg
2 tablespoons caster sugar
½ pint milk
1 oz gelatine
½ pint double cream
arrowroot (for thickening juice)

6-inch cake tin, or charlotte tin

Method
Oil the mould. String the currants and put them into a pan with sugar to taste. Cover pan, and set on low heat for 15-20 minutes, until currants are completely tender. Drain off the juice and reserve. Rub currants through a nylon strainer and measure resulting purée. There should be between ½ - ¾ pint. If too thick, dilute with a little juice to the consistency of cream.

Cream egg yolks and the whole egg together with the sugar. Bring milk to the boil, pour on to the egg and sugar and blend well; set aside to cool.

Soak the gelatine in a wineglass of redcurrant juice or water, dissolve over gentle heat and add to the custard. Stir in the purée gradually.

Watchpoint When using an acid fruit such as this make sure that the purée is sweet enough before it is added to the other ingredients; or it may start to ferment if kept 4-5 hours.

Partially whip the cream and fold in to the custard purée mixture before turning into the mould. Cover and leave in refrigerator for 1 hour or longer. When set, turn out. Thicken reserved juice slightly with arrowroot, then let it cool; pour this sauce round the cream.

Crème blanche
with cranberry compote

1 pint milk
2 tablespoons granulated sugar
1 vanilla pod
5 egg whites
½ pint double cream

For cranberry compote
1 lb cranberries
sugar syrup (made from ½ pint water and 8 oz granulated sugar)
1 lb dessert apples

6-inch diameter (No. 2 size) soufflé dish

Method
Set the oven at 375°F or Mark 5. Put the milk, sugar and vanilla pod in a pan and heat gently until the sugar is dissolved; cover and leave to infuse for 5 minutes. Lightly whisk the egg whites with a fork, just enough to make them smooth but not fluffy: strain on the milk and leave to cool. Then add half the cream. Pour mixture into the soufflé dish, cover with greaseproof paper or foil and cook in the pre-set oven for about 35-40 minutes in a bain-marie until set. Leave until cold. Turn out, mask with remaining cream, lightly whipped.

To make the cranberry compote: make a syrup of the sugar and water, boiling it for only 2-3 minutes. Peel, quarter and core the apples, slice each in half. Add to the syrup, cover and poach gently for 15-20 minutes until tender. Draw pan aside and leave uncovered until cool.

Carefully lift out apples into a dish, reboil syrup, add cranberries; simmer for 5 minutes, then pour over apples. Chill before serving.

Serve crème blanche with a cranberry compote for a contrast of
colour and flavour

Gooseberry cream

1 lb gooseberries
½ pint water
3 tablespoons granulated sugar
scant 1 oz gelatine
½ pint double cream
1½ tablespoons caster sugar
2-3 drops edible green colouring

For decoration
1 pint lemon jelly (see page 72)
pistachio nuts, or small diamonds
  of angelica

*6-7 inch diameter cake tin, or
charlotte tin*

Method
Top and tail the gooseberries
and poach them until tender in
a syrup made from the water and
granulated sugar; then drain
and rub fruit through a nylon
sieve. Set this purée and ½ pint
of the syrup on one side.

Line the mould with the cold
but still liquid jelly, decorate the
bottom with pistachio nuts (or
angelica), setting the decoration in sufficient jelly to cover.

Add half of the reserved
syrup to the gelatine, allow it
to soak and then dissolve it over
gentle heat. Half whip the
cream in a bowl, add the fruit
purée, remaining syrup, sugar
and colouring. Add the melted
gelatine, stir gently with the
bowl set on ice cubes until
cream begins to thicken, then
pour it at once into the prepared
mould. Leave it to set firm.

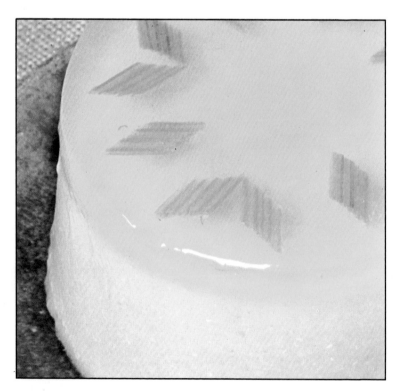

Crème Margot

¼ pint strawberry purée
½ oz gelatine
3 tablespoons water
3 tablespoons double cream
   (whipped)
1 egg white (stiffly whisked)

For custard
3 egg yolks
1½ oz caster sugar
½ pint milk

For decoration
whole strawberries
few pistachio nuts
little double cream

Method

Purée strawberries by rubbing through a nylon strainer.

Work the egg yolks and sugar together until light in colour. Scald milk, then pour it on to the egg mixture. Return mixture to the pan and stir it over gentle heat until the custard coats the back of the spoon; do not boil it. Strain this custard and leave it to cool.

Soak the gelatine in the water, then dissolve it over gentle heat and add to the custard with the strawberry purée. Place the bowl over ice and stir until custard is thickening creamily, then fold in the cream and the egg white. Turn into a glass bowl to set.

Decorate it with whipped cream, whole strawberries and pistachio nuts.

Petits pots de crème

A simple and delicious sweet (see photograph page 129). Cook the same way as for Crème caramel (page 138). Little, deep mousse pots made in oven-proof china should be used, otherwise ramekin pots will do. Made in a variety of flavours and arranged on a large dish these 'petits pots' look good on a buffet table. Serve plain or with cream.

The basic ingredients are 1½ pints of milk, 3 eggs and 3 egg yolks, and 3 tablespoons caster sugar. The following flavourings may be added, adjusting the recipe where necessary:

For chocolate flavour: simmer 2 oz plain dessert chocolate in ½ pint milk for 2-3 minutes. Then pour on to 1 egg, 1 egg yolk and 1 tablespoon of caster sugar which have been beaten together. Blend, strain and pour into pots.

For coffee flavour: dissolve 2 teaspoons instant coffee in ½ pint hot milk; make custard as for chocolate flavour.

For vanilla flavour: infuse the milk with a vanilla pod and use vanilla sugar in place of caster sugar. When well flavoured, mix with the beaten eggs and continue to make as for the chocolate flavour.

When the pots are full, set them in water in a bain-marie, or in a deep ovenproof dish on a baking sheet, covered with buttered paper; cook in oven at 350-375°F or Mark 4-5 for 12-15 minutes until just set. Take out and chill.

Crème caramel with strawberry sauce

6 oz lump, or granulated, sugar
¼ pint water
1 pint milk
1 tablespoon granulated sugar
2 eggs
2 egg yolks
½ lb strawberries
2-3 tablespoons caster, or icing, sugar

6-inch diameter charlotte tin (1½ pints capacity), or No. 2 size soufflé dish

Method

Put the 6 oz sugar and half the water in a heavy pan and dissolve over gentle heat, then boil it steadily to a rich brown caramel. Pour in the remaining water (taking care to cover your hand against any splashes) and stir carefully until all the caramel is dissolved; then pour it into a bowl to cool. Set oven at 375°F or Mark 5.

Warm the milk with 1 tablespoon sugar and stir until it is dissolved. Break the eggs and yolks with a fork; do not whisk or make them frothy but just beat them enough to make them smooth. Pour on the warm milk, then stir in the caramel. Strain this mixture into the lightly oiled tin or dish and cover with foil or greaseproof paper. Cook custard au bain-marie in pre-set oven for about 45 minutes until set.

Meanwhile hull and slice the strawberries, dust with some caster (or icing) sugar and leave for 30 minutes. Rub the fruit through a nylon strainer and sweeten with the remaining sugar. Allow the custard to stand about 30 minutes before turning on to a serving dish. Pour the strawberry sauce around when the custard is cold.

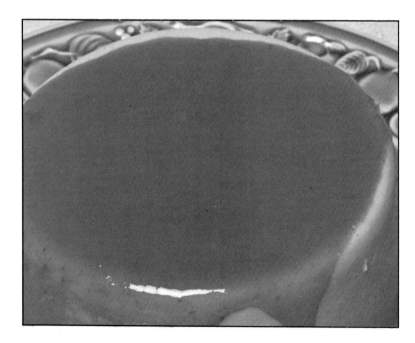

Meringues

Meringues and fruit — nothing could be more delicious. For a perfect summer dessert at a time when fruit is a little scarce and expensive, try eeking it out with meringue shells, or scattering the fruit over the top of meringue baskets already filled with cream.

Meringue has a particular quality of smooth sweetness, completely unmarred by any stickiness, that is unlike anything else in the culinary field. And its texture is part of the enjoyment.

Basically egg white and sugar, there are three different kinds of meringue. **Meringue suisse** is made with egg white and caster sugar; **meringue cuite** is made with icing sugar, and a slightly higher proportion of sugar per egg white; **meringue italienne** is made with lump sugar, dis-

solved to a syrup and boiled before being added to the egg whites. Meringue italienne is the lightest, finest mixture but because it requires a sugar thermometer it is rarely used in the home when the other methods are so much simpler. It is really more for professionals, engaged in pâtisserie work.

To ensure a uniform result for meringues, it is important to weigh the sugar accurately. And for meringue suisse you will get a better volume of egg white and a fluffier meringue if you whisk the egg by hand with a balloon whisk. A rounded copper bowl, which fits the shape of the whisk will also help. With a rotary whisk or electric mixer, there is a risk of overbeating. For meringue cuite, or italienne, however, use a rotary whisk in a pudding basin, or an electric mixer.

Filled with fresh fruit and cream or ice-cream just before serving, this large meringue basket makes an attractive and delicious summer sweet for 6-8 people. See right for instructions on how to make it

Strawberry meringue baskets

For meringue cuite
8½ oz icing sugar
4 egg whites
3 drops of vanilla essence

For filling
8 oz small fresh strawberries
2 tablespoons redcurrant jelly (see page 155)

Baking sheet lined with non-stick (silicone) cooking, or rice, paper ; nylon forcing bag with 8-cut vegetable rose pipe

Method
Set oven at 275-300°F or Mark 1-2. Rub icing sugar through a nylon strainer on to a sheet of greaseproof paper ; have ready a pan half-full of gently simmering water.

Put the egg whites in a pudding basin, beat until foaming with a rotary or electric beater, then add the icing sugar, 1 tablespoon at a time. When all the icing sugar has been added, flavour with vanilla essence, set the basin on the pan of hot water (unless using an electric beater) and continue beating until the mixture holds its schape.

To test, lift a little of the mixture on the whisk and let it fall. If ready, it will retain its shape as a thick ribbon when it falls in the basin.

Fill the mixture into a nylon forcing bag. Shape into 6 small baskets, bake for 45 minutes in pre-set oven. Allow to cool.

Beat redcurrant jelly in a basin with a small whisk or fork and rub through a strainer into a pan ; heat gently until clear. Hull the strawberries and turn very gently in the warm redcurrant glaze until evenly coated. Spoon into baskets.

Large meringue basket

For a 7-inch diameter basket that will give 6-8 portions, you will need double the quantity of ingredients as in recipe for small strawberry meringue baskets (left). Make it in two batches because you will find one large batch too much to cope with. ·

Method
Set the oven at 275°F or Mark 1, line 2 baking sheets with non-stick (silicone) cooking paper.

Make up first batch of meringue cuite and put about half in a forcing bag fitted with a ½-inch éclair pipe. Use about two-thirds of this to shape one round, 6 inches in diameter, and one hoop of the same size. Bake for 45-50 minutes until dry and crisp. During this baking time keep the basin of remaining meringue mixture covered with a damp cloth to stop it from hardening in the basin.

When the round and hoop are ready, turn on to a wire rack to cool and peel off the non-stick paper. Turn this paper over, put back on to the baking sheets and pipe two more hoops of the meringue to the same size as before. Bake and cool as before.

Make up the second batch of meringue and use a little of this uncooked mixture to mount the hoops on the round, one on top of the other. Now put the rest of mixture in a forcing bag fitted with an 8-cut vegetable rose pipe and cover the plainly piped hoops with a decorative pattern (see left). Bake again at the same temperature for 45-50 minutes until set and crisp.

This meringue case can be made at least a week before a party and stored in an airtight ▶

Large meringue baskets continued

container. Fill with fresh fruit and cream, or ice-cream, just before serving.

1 *Draw 6-inch circle on non-stick (silicone) cooking paper to act as piping guide for a meringue basket. Use ½-inch éclair pipe*
2 *Pipe three hoops of the same diameter (in two batches). When baked and cool, mount on circular base of the basket*
3 *With more meringue mixture, pipe decoration on to hoops ; bake again, and fill with fruit and cream*

Pavlova

4 **egg whites**
$\frac{1}{4}$ **teaspoon salt**
8 **oz caster sugar**
4 **teaspoons cornflour**
2 **teaspoons vinegar**
$\frac{1}{2}$ **teaspoon vanilla essence**
$\frac{1}{2}$ **pint double cream**
a **selection of fresh fruit, or**
   canned fruit salad

9-inch diameter shallow oven-proof dish

Method
Set the oven at 275°F or Mark 1. Beat the egg whites and salt with a rotary whisk or electric mixer until stiff. Add the sugar, 1 tablespoon at a time, whisking until very stiff, then beat in the cornflour, vinegar and vanilla. Butter a shallow ovenproof dish, fill with the meringue mixture; hollow out the centre somewhat.

Bake for $1\frac{1}{4}$ hours in the slow pre-set oven. When cool fill with sweetened and flavoured cream and fresh fruit.

Note : in Australia this is served filled with a little fresh whipped cream and a lot of tropical fruit : banana, mixed with passion fruit and sometimes fresh pineapple or pawpaw. We increase the quantity of cream to $\frac{1}{2}$ pint. To give the same authentic flavour, tropical fruit salad (canned in Australia) could be served separately.

Apricot suédoise with meringues

½ lb dried apricots, soaked overnight in 1½ pints boiling water
strip of lemon rind
4 oz granulated sugar
1 rounded tablespoon gelatine
¼ pint water
½ pint double cream
vanilla flavouring

For meringues
2 egg whites
4 oz caster sugar

*6-inch diameter soufflé dish, or cake
   tin*

*A steady hand and even piping will
give you perfect meringues — so do
take your time*

Method

Cook the apricots with the lemon
rind in the liquid in which they
were soaked until very soft, then
rub through a sieve or strainer.
Measure the purée and make up
to 1½ pints with water. Return to
the pan with the sugar and
simmer 5-10 minutes. Soak the
gelatine in the water and then
dissolve over heat. Add to the
fruit purée and allow to cool.
Pour into a wet soufflé dish or
cake tin and leave to set in refrigerator for several hours.

To prepare meringues : whisk
egg whites until stiff. Whisk 1
dessertspoon of the sugar into
the whites for 1 minute, or until
the mixture looks like satin. Fold
the remaining sugar in with a
metal spoon.

Spoon blobs of mixture (about
the size of a penny) on to a
baking sheet lined with non-stick
(silicone) cooking paper, and
flick up mixture into peaks, or

pipe into small meringues. Bake for 45 minutes in a low oven at 250°F or Mark $\frac{1}{2}$ until dry and crisp.

Turn the jelly on to a serving dish and cover first with whipped cream flavoured with vanilla, then with meringues.

Suédoise usually means a sweet fruit purée set with gelatine, put into a mould and served with cream or custard.

Dacquoise

3 oz almonds
4 egg whites
8 oz caster sugar
pinch of cream of tartar

For filling
4 oz dried apricots (soaked
    overnight in water)
strip of lemon rind
4 oz granulated sugar
$\frac{1}{4}$ pint water
juice of $\frac{1}{2}$ lemon
$\frac{1}{2}$ pint double cream
sugar (to taste)

For decoration
2 tablespoons icing sugar (sifted)
1 oz plain block chocolate (grated)
extra double cream

*2 baking sheets lined with non-stick
    (silicone) kitchen paper*

Method
Set the oven at 275°F or Mark 1.
Blanch almonds (see page 154),
dry well and pass them through
a nut mill.

Watchpoint It is important for
this recipe that the almonds are
juicy and freshly ground, so if
you have only ready-blanched
almonds in your store cupboard,
pour boiling water over them
and leave them to soak for 10
minutes.

Whisk the egg whites until
stiff, add 1 tablespoon of the
caster sugar and the cream of
tartar and continue whisking for
1 minute. Fold in the remaining
caster sugar and the prepared
almonds.

Divide the mixture between
the baking sheets and spread
carefully into two rounds, 8

*To test if dacquoise is done, lift
corner of paper ; if it peels away,
mixture is ready*

*Filling dacquoise with whipped
cream and a little of the apricot
purée to flavour*

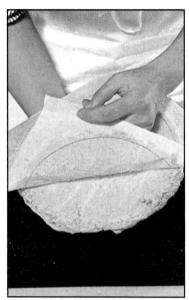

146

inches in diameter. Bake for about 1 hour in the pre-set oven. To test if the dacquoise is done, lift the corner of the paper and if it peels away from the bottom the mixture is ready (if not, continue baking until this happens). Leave to cool.

Stew the apricots gently in their soaking liquid with a strip of lemon rind to flavour. When tender, rub apricots through a fine sieve and leave them to cool.

Dissolve the granulated sugar in the water, add the lemon juice and boil for 3 minutes to make a sugar syrup. Whip the cream, sweeten to taste, and mix in a little of the apricot purée to flavour (about a quarter to a third) ; put into the dacquoise. Dust the top with icing sugar and decorate with rosettes of cream and grated chocolate. Dilute the remaining apricot purée with the sugar syrup and serve this sauce separately.

Finished dacquoise decorated with rosettes of cream and grated chocolate ; the apricot sauce is served separately in a sauce boat

Strawberry japonais

3 oz ground almonds
6 oz caster sugar
3 egg whites
8 oz coffee-flavoured fondant,
 or glacé, icing (see pages 153-154)
$\frac{1}{2}$ lb strawberries
$\frac{1}{4}$ pint double cream
vanilla essence
1 oz ground almonds (browned) —
 see page 154

Method
Set oven at 275-325°F or Mark 1-3: Mix the 3 oz of ground almonds and 6 oz sugar together and pass them through a wire sieve or strainer to make sure they are thoroughly blended. Whisk the egg whites until stiff, then fold in the almond and sugar mixture.

Divide this meringue mixture in two and spread into 6-6$\frac{1}{2}$ inch rounds on two baking sheets lined with non-stick kitchen paper. Bake in pre-set oven for about 50-60 minutes and then lift almond meringue carefully on to a cooling rack ; turn it over to peel off the kitchen paper and then leave it to cool.

Coat one round of the almond meringue with coffee-flavoured icing. Reserve a few strawberries for decoration ; slice the rest and dust them with a little caster sugar.

Covering a round of japonais with the coffee-flavoured icing. Sugared strawberries are ready for the filling

Spooning strawberries on to the plain round of japonais which has been covered with whipped cream

148

Lightly whip the cream, sweeten it with 1 teaspoon caster sugar and flavour with vanilla essence. Spoon the cream on to the plain round of japonais and cover with the sliced strawberries. Place the iced round on top of this filling and press the browned ground almonds around the sides. Decorate the top with the whole strawberries.

The decorated strawberry japonais

Hazelnut meringue cake
with Melba sauce

4 egg whites
9 oz caster sugar
3-4 drops of vanilla essence
½ teaspoon vinegar
4½ oz hazelnuts (shelled, browned and ground)
½ pint double cream
½ lb raspberries (optional)
icing sugar (for dusting)

Two 8-inch diameter sandwich tins

Method

Butter and flour the sides of the sandwich tins and line the bottom with a disc of non-stick (silicone) cooking paper. Set the oven at 375°F or Mark 5.

Whisk the egg whites until stiff with a rotary or electric beater, add the sugar 1 tablespoon at a time and continue beating until the mixture is very stiff and stands in peaks. Whisk in the vanilla essence and vinegar, then fold in prepared nuts.

Divide the mixture between the two prepared tins and smooth the top with a palette knife; bake 30-40 minutes but no longer. The top of the meringue will be crisp and the inside soft like a marshmallow. Turn on to wire racks to cool.

Watchpoint Always fill meringue at least three hours before serving; cake will then cut into portions without splintering.

Whisk the cream, sweeten and flavour with extra sugar and vanilla; use about two-thirds to fill meringue. If wished, add raspberries to the cream filling, reserving some for decoration. Dust top with icing sugar and use the remaining cream to shape, or pipe, rosettes on the top. Serve Melba sauce separately (see page 28).

To fill the meringue rounds, first whisk the cream (top left), then add sugar and flavour it with vanilla essence. Spoon in over half of the cream, leaving some for decoration

150

Appendix

Notes and basic recipes

Apricot jam sauce

2 rounded tablespoons of home-
    made apricot jam
about 7½ fl oz water
2 strips of lemon rind
1 tablespoon sugar
1 tablespoon arrowroot (slaked
    with 1 tablespoon water) —
    optional

Method
Put all the ingredients, except the
arrowroot, into a pan and bring
slowly to the boil, stirring well.
Taste, and if not strong enough in
flavour add a little more jam.
Continue to simmer for 5-6 minutes,
then remove the lemon rind and
thicken if necessary with the arrowroot. Serve hot.

Baking blind

A flan case should be pre-cooked
before filling with soft or cooked
fruit. Once the flan ring is lined with
pastry, chill for about 30 minutes
to ensure the dough is well set.

Now line the pastry with crumpled
greaseproof paper, pressing it well
into the dough at the bottom edge
and sides.

Three-parts fill the flan with uncooked rice or beans (to hold the
shape) and put into the oven to
bake. An 8-inch diameter flan ring
holding a 6-8 oz quantity of pastry
should cook for about 26 minutes
in an oven at 400°F or Mark 6.

After about 20 minutes of the
cooking time take flan out of the
oven and carefully remove the paper
and rice, or beans. (Rice, or beans,
may be used many times over for
baking blind.) Replace the flan in
the oven to complete cooking. The
ring itself can either be taken off
with the paper and rice, or removed
after cooking. Once cooked, slide
the flan on to a wire rack and then
leave to cool.

Breadcrumbs

To make crumbs : take a large loaf
(the best type to use is a sandwich
loaf) at least two days old. Cut off
the crust and keep to one side.
Break up bread into crumbs either
by rubbing through a wire sieve or
a Mouli sieve, or by working in an
electric blender.

Spread crumbs on to a sheet of
paper laid on a baking tin and cover
with another sheet of paper to keep
off any dust. Leave to dry in a warm
temperature — the plate rack, or
warming drawer, or the top of the
oven, or even the airing cupboard,
is ideal. The crumbs may take a day
or two to dry thoroughly, and they
must be crisp before storing in a
jar. To make them uniformly fine,
sift them through a wire bowl strainer.

To make browned crumbs : bake
the crusts in a slow oven until
golden-brown, then crush or grind
through a mincer. Sift and store as
for white crumbs. These browned
ones are known as raspings and are
used for any dish that is coated with
a sauce and browned in the oven.

Butter cream

2 oz granulated sugar
4 tablespoons water
2 egg yolks
6 oz unsalted butter

Method
Dissolve the sugar in water in a
saucepan over gentle heat, then
boil it steadily until the cooled syrup
forms a 'thread' between the finger
and thumb (216-218°F on a sugar
thermometer).
Watchpoint To test between the
finger and thumb, remove a little
syrup from the pan, off the heat,
with the handle of a teaspoon, then
test.

When bubbles subside pour the syrup on to the egg yolks and whisk until mixture is thick and mousse-like. Cream the butter until soft and add the egg mousse gradually. Flavour to taste with melted sweetened chocolate, or coffee essence, or the zest of orange or lemon rind and use as required.

Chantilly cream

Turn ½ pint of double cream into a cold basin and, using a fork or open wire whisk, whisk gently until it thickens. Add 3-4 teaspoons caster sugar to taste and 2-3 drops of vanilla essence and continue whisking until the cream will hold its shape.

For a delicate flavour, instead of the essence, sweeten with vanilla sugar and a few of the seeds scraped from a vanilla pod.

Chocolate caraque

Grate 3 oz plain block chocolate or chocolate couverture (cooking chocolate). Melt on a plate over hot water and work with a palette knife until smooth. Spread this thinly on a marble slab or laminated surface and leave until nearly set. Then, using a long sharp knife, shave it off the slab, slantwise, using a slight sawing movement and holding the knife almost upright. The chocolate will form long scrolls or flakes. These will keep in an airtight tin but look better when they are freshly made.

Chocolate sauce

2 oz plain block chocolate
2 tablespoons sugar
1 teaspoon cocoa
1 teaspoon instant coffee
½ pint water
1 egg yolk (optional)
½ teaspoon vanilla essence

Method
Break up the chocolate and put into a saucepan with the sugar, cocoa, coffee and water. Heat slowly, stirring frequently until dissolved. Then simmer with the lid off the pan until it is the consistency of thin cream.

Draw pan aside, and if using the yolk, blend with 1-2 tablespoons of the hot sauce before adding it to the pan, and then add the vanilla essence. If no yolk is used, continue to simmer the sauce until it is a little thicker before adding vanilla.

Fondant icing

1 lb lump sugar
8 tablespoons water
pinch of cream of tartar

A sugar thermometer is essential for this recipe.

You can now buy blocks or packets of powder of fondant icing. Simply follow the manufacturer's instructions.

Method
Place the sugar and water in a saucepan and dissolve, without stirring, over a low heat. Using a brush dipped in cold water, wipe round pan at level of the syrup to prevent a crust forming. Add the cream of tartar (dissolved in 1 teaspoon of water), place the lid on the pan, increase the heat and bring to the boil.

Remove the lid after 2 minutes, put a sugar thermometer in and boil the syrup steadily to 240°F. When it has reached this temperature take the pan off the heat at once, wait for the bubbles to subside then pour the mixture very slowly on to a damp marble or laminated plastic slab. Work with a wooden spatula until it becomes a firm and white fondant. Take a small piece of fondant at a time and knead with the fingertips until smooth.

For storing, pack fondant icing in an airtight jar or tin. When you want to use it, gently warm the fondant with a little sugar syrup to make a smooth cream. The icing should then flow easily. Flavour and colour it just before use with vanilla, lemon, etc. Spread over cake with a palette knife.

French flan pastry

4 oz plain flour
pinch of salt
2 oz butter
2 oz caster sugar
2-3 drops of vanilla essence
2 egg yolks

This quantity is sufficient to line a 7-inch diameter flan ring or 9-12 individual tartlet tins, according to size.
Note : 2 oz vanilla sugar may be used instead of caster sugar and vanilla essence.

Method
Sieve the flour with a pinch of salt on to a marble slab or pastry board, make a well in the centre and in it place the butter, sugar, vanilla essence and egg yolks. Using the fingertips of one hand only, pinch and work these last three ingredients together until well blended. Then draw in the flour, knead lightly until smooth. (See photographs, pages 104-105).

Make the French flan pastry 1-2 hours before using, then chill.

Gelatine
The best gelatine is obtained from simmering calves feet in water and is especially delicate in flavour. Most powdered gelatine is obtained from the bones or tissues of animals or fish by boiling. Always use a good quality gelatine and check the amount required with manufacturers' directions.

Glacé icing

4-5 tablespoons granulated sugar
$\frac{1}{4}$ pint water
8-12 oz icing sugar (finely sifted)
flavouring essence and colouring
(as required)

Method
Make sugar syrup by dissolving sugar in $\frac{1}{4}$ pint of water in a small saucepan. Bring to the boil, and boil steadily for 10 minutes. Remove pan from the heat and when quite cold, add the icing sugar, 1 tablespoon at a time, and beat thoroughly with a wooden spatula. The icing should coat back of spoon and look very glossy. Warm the pan gently on a very low heat. **Watchpoint** The pan must not get too hot. You should be able to touch the bottom with the palm of your hand.

Flavour and colour icing; spread over cake with palette knife.

Nuts
To brown hazelnuts (already shelled) : do not blanch first but bake for 7-8 minutes in a moderate oven at 350 °F or Mark 4, then rub briskly in a rough cloth to remove skin.

Almonds : buy them with their skins on. This way they retain their oil better. Blanching to remove the skins gives extra juiciness.

To blanch almonds : pour boiling water over the shelled nuts, cover the pan and leave until cool. Then the skins can be easily removed (test one with finger and thumb). Drain, rinse in cold water ; press skins off with fingers. Rinse, dry thoroughly.

To brown almonds : blanch, and bake as for hazelnuts (left).

To chop almonds : first blanch, skin, chop and then brown them in the oven, if desired.

To shred almonds : first blanch, skin, split in two and cut each half lengthways in fine pieces. These can then be used as they are or browned quickly in the oven, with or without a sprinkling of caster sugar.

To flake almonds : first blanch and skin, then cut horizontally into flakes with a small sharp knife.

To grind almonds : first blanch, then skin, chop and pound into a paste (use a pestle and mortar, or a grinder, or the butt end of a rolling pin). Home-prepared ground almonds taste much better than the ready-ground variety.

To blanch pistachio nuts : treat as for almonds, but add a pinch of bicarbonate of soda to the water to preserve the colour of the nuts.

Puff pastry

8 oz plain flour
pinch of salt
8 oz butter
1 teaspoon lemon juice
scant $\frac{1}{4}$ pint water (ice cold)

Method
Sift flour and salt into a bowl. Rub in a piece of butter the size of a walnut. Add lemon juice to water, make a well in centre of flour and pour in about two-thirds of the liquid. Mix with a palette, or round-bladed, knife. When the dough is beginning to form, add remaining water.

Turn out the dough on to a marble slab, a laminated-plastic work top, or a board, dusted with flour. Knead dough for 2-3 minutes, then roll out to a square about $\frac{1}{2}$-$\frac{3}{4}$ inch thick.

Beat butter, if necessary, to make it pliable and place in centre of dough. Fold this up over butter to enclose it completely (sides and ends over centre like a parcel). Wrap in a cloth or piece of grease-proof paper and put in the refrigerator for 10-15 minutes.

Flour slab or work top, put on dough, the join facing upwards, and bring rolling pin down on to dough 3-4 times to flatten it slightly.

Now roll out to a rectangle about $\frac{1}{2}$-$\frac{3}{4}$ inch thick. Fold into three, ends to middle, as accurately as possible, if necessary pulling the ends to keep them rectangular. Seal the edges with your hand or rolling pin and turn pastry half round to bring the edge towards you. Roll out again and fold in three (keep a note of the 'turns' given). Set pastry aside in refrigerator for 15 minutes.

Repeat this process, giving a total of 6 turns with a 15-minute rest after each two turns. Then leave in the refrigerator until wanted.
Watchpoint Always roll the dough away from you, keeping the pressure as even as possible.

Redcurrant jelly

It is not possible to give a specific quantity of redcurrants as the recipe is governed by the amount of juice made, which is variable.

Method
Wash the fruit and, without removing from the stems, put in a 7 lb jam jar or stone crock. Cover and stand in deep pan of hot water. Simmer on top of the stove or in the oven at 350°F or Mark 4, mashing the fruit a little from time to time, until all the juice is extracted (about 1 hour).

Then turn fruit into a jelly-bag, or double linen strainer, and allow to drain undisturbed overnight over a basin.

155

Watchpoint To keep the jelly clear and sparkling, do not try to speed up the draining process by forcing juice through ; this will only make the jelly cloudy.

Now measure juice. Allowing 1 lb lump or preserving sugar to each pint of juice, mix juice and sugar together, dissolving over slow heat. When dissolved, bring to the boil, boil hard for 3-5 minutes and skim with a wooden spoon. Test a little on a saucer : allow jelly to cool, tilt saucer and, if jelly is set, it will wrinkle. Put into jam jars, place small circles of greaseproof paper over jelly, label and cover with jam pot covers. Store in a dry larder until required.

Rich shortcrust pastry

8 oz plain flour
pinch of salt
6 oz butter
1 rounded dessertspoon caster sugar (for sweet pastry)
1 egg yolk
2-3 tablespoons cold water

Method
Sift the flour with a pinch of salt into a mixing bowl. Drop in the butter and cut it into the flour until the small pieces are well coated. Then rub them in with the fingertips until the mixture looks like fine breadcrumbs. Stir in the sugar, mix egg yolk with water, tip into the fat and flour and mix quickly with a palette knife to a firm dough.

Turn on to a floured board and knead lightly till smooth. If possible, chill in refrigerator (wrapped in greaseproof paper, a polythene bag or foil) for 30 minutes before using.

Shortcrust pastry

8 oz plain flour
pinch of salt
4-6 oz butter, margarine, lard or shortening (one of the commercially prepared fats), or a mixture of any two
3-4 tablespoons cold water

Method
Sift the flour with a pinch of salt into a mixing bowl. Cut the fat into the flour with a round-bladed knife and, as soon as the pieces are well coated with flour, rub in with the fingertips until the mixture looks like fine breadcrumbs.

Make a well in the centre, add the water (reserving about 1 tablespoon) and mix quickly with a knife. Press together with the fingers, adding the extra water, if necessary, to give a firm dough.

Turn on to a floured board, knead pastry lightly until smooth. Chill in refrigerator (wrapped in greaseproof paper, a polythene bag, or foil) for 30 minutes before using.

Note : when terms such as 8 oz pastry or an 8 oz quantity of pastry are used, this means the amount obtained by using 8 oz of flour, not 8 oz of prepared dough. As a quantity guide, 8 oz of shortcrust pastry will cover a 9-inch long pie dish holding 1½ lb of fruit, or line an 8-inch flan ring. For a covered plate pie (8-9 inches in diameter), 10 oz of shortcrust pastry would be required.

Glossary

Bain-Marie (au) To cook at temperature just below boiling point in a bain-marie (a saucepan standing in a larger pan of simmering water). Used in the preparation of sauces, creams and foods liable to spoil if cooked over direct heat. May be carried out in oven or on top of stove. A double saucepan gives similar result. Sauces and other delicate dishes may be kept hot in a bain-marie at less than simmering heats.

Bake blind To pre-cook a pastry case before filling (see page 152 for method).

Caramelise 1 To dissolve sugar slowly in water, then boil steadily, without stirring, to a coffee-brown colour. **2** To give a thin caramel topping by dusting top of sweet with caster or icing sugar, and grilling slowly.

Hull To remove stalks and leaves from strawberries.

Infuse To steep in liquid (not always boiling) in warm place to draw the flavour into the liquid.

Macerate To soak / infuse, mostly fruit, in liqueur / syrup.

Ratafias Button-size macaroons, strongly flavoured with almonds.

Scald 1 To plunge into boiling water for easy peeling. **2** To heat a liquid, eg. milk, to just under boiling point.

Slake To mix a flour or other powder with a little cold water before adding to a larger quantity of liquid. This ensures that the powder blends evenly into the liquid, without forming lumps.

Vanilla sugar Sugar delicately flavoured with vanilla (made by storing 1-2 vanilla pods in a jar of sugar).

Index